WHAT CARRIES YOU

A Novel in the Form of a Memoir

By

Richard E. Welch III

Cover photo courtesy of Robert Marquand Welch

Printed in the United States of America
First Printing, 2019
ISBN 978-1-692-97179-3

Author Email: richard.e.welch3@gmail.com

"All life is largely based on the avoidance of fact."

- John P. Marquand

FOR:

JBW

RCW

RMW

With Endless Love

Contents

Preface xiii

Acknowledgements xv

Chapter One: *A Straightforward Job* 1

Chapter Two: *Summer Idyll* 11

Chapter Three: *Marseille* 27

Chapter Four: *The Running Dog* 35

Chapter Five: *Evening Things* 45

Chapter Six: *Distant Lands* 57

Chapter Seven: *Looking for Mr. Right* 69

Chapter Eight: *Way Up on Slough* 79

Chapter Nine: *A Hole You Never Fill* 103

Chapter Ten: *Memorial Day* 119

Chapter Eleven: *This Your Rig?* 125

Chapter Twelve: *The Sword from the Stone* 135

Chapter Thirteen: *Bedtime Stories* 149

Chapter Fourteen: *Striped Blast* 155

Chapter Fifteen: *Swimming the Grey's* 159

Chapter Sixteen: *Don't You Want to Be an Outlaw?* 165

Chapter Seventeen: *As Darkness Rolls Away* 181

Chapter Eighteen: *The Peaceable Kingdom* 189

Chapter Nineteen: *What Carries You Out* 197

About the Author 213

Preface

This short novel, as a disapproving publisher wrote Norman Maclean, "has trees in it." Not only trees, but rivers, mountains, and birds. If you dislike trees, or nature for that matter, you may wish to read no further.

I have been lucky to spend much of my free time outdoors doing things that require little mental effort. As one strolls through a forest, fishes for trout, kayaks a river, or climbs a mountain, one's mind tends to wander. The result of these mental wanderings was, first, a short story, and then, another. The stories began to become interwoven and take on a progression. The result was this novel. Sadly, this book is not autobiographical for it depicts a life much more interesting than my own.

Although this novel takes the form of a memoir, it truly is a work of fiction. Any writer uses his or her own experiences as a springboard into circumstances and characters that never existed except in the imaginary world of the author. As John P. Marquand explained nearly eighty years ago, "Living men and women are too limited, too far from being typical, too greatly lacking in any universal appeal, to serve in a properly planned piece of fiction. A successful character in a novel is a conglomerate, a combination of dozens of traits, drawn from experience with hundreds of individuals, many of them half known and half forgotten; and all these traits have been transformed by passing through the writer's mind." Let me put it less eloquently and more bluntly: if you think any character is based on someone you know, you are wrong. Only three persons have a right to complain that the characters hew too closely to reality, my two sons and my late, fine friend, Jack.

The novel is admittedly written on a small canvas. A white American male grows up. Remember, however, that there is drama in a backyard garden. What you get is a short tale about a life well lived: the friendships, the rough road to finding love, confronting death, and the challenging task of raising children. All while trying to fly fish as much as possible. I hope you enjoy it; trees, rivers, mountains, and all.

Acknowledgements

This book would not exist except for the help of many. There are four people I would particularly like to acknowledge. Elizabeth Marquand Welch, a talented and kind editor, reviewed this manuscript repeatedly making many corrections and improvements. Thank you. Any remaining errors are mine alone. Anthony Flaherty, who has no interest in fly fishing, kindly reviewed an earlier draft and made many helpful suggestions. Publication would not have been possible without the talents of Shanlynn Rabenda. She arranged all the formatting and navigated the technicalities—all of which were beyond my comprehension. The greatest thanks goes to my wife, Judith, who patiently listened to much of this book and suggested essential revisions. She kept me on the tracks.

Chapter One: *A Straightforward Job*

The broom stayed next to my mother's bed so that she could scare away the big river rats that crawled up through the old mill works. Usually the vermin, including the occasional bat from the rafters, had the decency to await my mother down on the first floor. Armed with the broom, the handle thumping on the floor, she walked down the stairs each morning filled with fear, but ready to do battle. It was the occasional otter, still eating a carp, that really set her off. Her five children and her husband were light burdens compared to this.

The sound of the broom handle and my mother's loud chanting, "Here I come, I hate you, Yes I do," would wake me most summer mornings. Never does a day hold more promise than a summer day in childhood. It is a day blessedly free of the fear or boredom of school. It is another day to wander, to linger, like the slow stream that flowed under my home.

An eight-year-old child remembers everything: the smell of cigarette smoke and cheap cream sherry as your parents sat talking on the porch every night before dinner, the taste of watermelon as the shiny, brown seeds swirled against your tongue and into your cheek before you pursed your lips and spit them out in a long stream, the bumper sticker attached with wire onto the family Bel Air station wagon that read Kennedy/Johnson, and the sound of your mother scattering pots in a metal drawer when searching for the frying pan. You remember Sunday mornings when your father, wearing your mother's stained apron, made breakfast, doled out donuts and favorite sections of the Sunday paper to each child, delivered the meal on a tray to your mother propped up and smiling in bed, and changed the bed sheets in each room while humming along to a Judy Garland record spinning on a small portable player.

Summer days lounge, the cicadas buzz high in the locust trees, the water over the mill dam barely trickles, the oaks cast a deep shade, and the humidity gives everything a slight mustiness. You remember it all, including the sound of handcuffs being snapped on your father's wrists.

Even at the age of eight, I must have had some persuasive powers, for I convinced my father, dressed in a suit and tie, to delay his trip to Harvard's Weidner Library to accompany me down to the concrete mill dam and watch me fish. Being a college professor, he spent three days a week in the summer traveling to Boston or Cambridge to research and the remaining four days writing in a small attic room. What he did was a mystery to me then, but he seemed happy and was always willing to join me on a wobbly canoe paddle when he returned or a walk through the woods before leaving. It seemed the perfect amount of time to spend with a father who had no talent as a fisherman or wilderness explorer. While my father was no Daniel Boone, I liked his warm presence as he sat beside me on the edge of the dam and I lobbed out my hook baited with a strip of baloney and a bobber made from a sherry bottle cork. I would examine the small scar on his cheek, his blue eyes, his short black hair, his frequent smile. And I liked his smell, like warm butter, as he sat beside me. It was all so familiar. What we talked about barely mattered, but it filled me with happiness to be beside the water, staring at my cork bobber, and talking with my dad.

We were not alone. On the concrete block at the middle of the mill dam spillway were two young men, one stocky and the other lean and gangly, fishing with spinning rods. This was not surprising, for our dam was known around town as the best place to cast into the pickerel rich mill pond.

A bright red bird with black wings flew in front of us, and I asked my father what type of bird it was.

"I haven't the slightest idea. Your mother might know. But, isn't it a pretty bird?"

I agreed.

After a bit, my mother came out of the mill, still wearing her apron, and walked over the bridge to where we sat.

"Dick, I'll watch him from the kitchen. You probably need to get going. Rich, your father needs to go to the city now."

Suddenly the stocky man on the dam block spoke to his friend. His voice was not loud, but with the water washing over the dam, he needed to raise his volume a bit in order to be heard. "Christ, they sound English. Are you hearing this shit, 'pretty bird' and 'go to the city'?"

The gangly man, "Yeah, and dig the suit and apron."

They both laughed.

My father had grown up in this small New England town but, upon hearing himself on tape, joked that he sounded like an English butler in a grade B movie. My mother had grown up on Beacon Hill and sounded like it. Until I left home for college, I never noticed their accents. Once I returned home, though, I realized that their voices sounded so different from the South Boston accents hyped in Hollywood that you would have thought of them as being from another continent. My father smiled at my mother and said in a surprisingly loud voice, "That's all right. I'm going to stay here for a minute more."

The stocky man now turned toward us and called to my father, "A minute more! What the fuck, buddy. Where do you come from?"

My father's warm, easy presence vanished. He no longer smelled like butter, but a stronger, bitter smell. He stood and told the men that they were on private property and to please keep their voices down.

The stocky man laughed, "Get a load of this shit."

My mother whispered that we should ignore the men and predicted that they would leave if we went back into the mill.

My father did not take her advice. "I'll have to ask you two to leave immediately."

"Why don't you make us leave?"

Sitting there with my fishing rod, I felt as though a cloud had settled over the day. I watched my father's dress shoes quickly move across the damp spillway to the concrete block. He was suddenly on the block with the two men as if by magic, and my mother was beside me.

"I have asked you to leave. You are trespassing. Now go."

The stocky man, who seemed much younger and stronger than my father, laughed again, leaned forward, and yelled "Fuck you!" in his face. I had never heard this phrase, but it was easy to understand that it was insulting.

Children love to recall their father doing some task requiring almost superhuman strength or acting in some heroic manner. But this was not that type of memory because it occurred too quickly.

The stocky man began to reach for my father or, at least, he dropped his rod. Suddenly my father's right fist blurred into a fast, upward arc. The man fell straight backward, and his head bounced on the concrete.

My mother made some sort of noise, and I felt cold.

"Holy shit!" cried the other man.

He bent over his friend. My father just stood there while the gangly man slowly rose. "You knocked him out. Do you know who he is?"

My father's tone was almost tranquil, "I have no idea who he is. But you better make sure he doesn't fall into the water."

"He's the police chief's younger brother!"

"Well," my father replied easily, "I think we better call the police chief. In the meantime, take care of your rude friend."

My father and mother urged me to go inside, but I slowly reeled in my line. My mother was crying and insisted that I leave immediately. My father put his arm around my mother and laughed, "Let him reel in. At least he has his priorities straight."

It had been a long time since I had seen the beautiful red bird with the black wings.

I did not go inside, but lurked with my next-door friend, Mark, in the bushes. The man on the block woke up about when the first police car arrived. The officer asked my father what had happened, and my father explained that the two men had been trespassing and using foul language.

The stocky man yelled up from the dam, "he sucker-punched me and almost killed me."

Mark and I crouched frozen with fascination.

The police officer called my father "sir," probably because he was wearing a suit and tie. But he didn't seem too friendly.

"Well, sir, even if he was trespassing and using what you call foul language, you don't have the right to punch him."

"Officer," my father replied in a calm and almost happy tone, "you might be correct. Still, I would do it again."

"Sir, I'm going to have to take you to the station."

My father smiled at the officer and said, "That's fine."

Mark whispered, "I think your dad is going to be arrested."

We stared at each other and then I heard, "Please hold out your hands."

The metal clinked and then snapped as the officer placed handcuffs on my father. My father looked out to the river with a slight smile on his face.

The police chief arrived next and hurried down to the dam to check on his brother. He took his brother's arm as they walked over the spillway. Then they talked quietly for a minute next to the chief's cruiser.

In the meantime, my mother looked at my father, clenched her hands, and said, "You look as though you are enjoying this. What is the matter with you?"

"Oh, dear," he replied sunnily, "I just enjoy a job well done. It's like being back in the service—a simple, straightforward fight. I never thought I would miss the Army, but maybe I do."

"But, Dick," my mother almost hissed, "You might end up down at the jail. It will probably be in the newspaper. You'll have to tell the college president. What if they bring charges?"

My father laughed softly. "Oh darling, it will all work out. That foul mouth deserved a bit of a lesson, and a little time in the slammer might be relaxing compared to five children." Although he was wearing handcuffs, my father stood straight and seemed light and carefree.

Mark whispered again, "Why's your dad so happy?"

My mother made an angry sound and stamped her right foot. Whenever my mother stamped her right foot, I knew she was really angry.

"Oh, Tina," my father responded, "don't be angry. I just think that a little incarceration might be a bit liberating."

"And leave me with all the children while you ruin your career?"

My father smiled broadly and began to laugh, bringing about another right foot stamp. "Oh, it won't come to that. And, I know you work much harder than I. How you do it all, I don't know. Truly, Tina, you are a hero. But I must admit that it is fun to think I might get a selfish vacation, and it's rather fun to think back on simpler times. You know, good guys and bad guys and all that. A time when I didn't need to be patient or to analyze things. My god, how children require patience. I miss a straight forward job."

Finally, my mother smiled slightly with the corners of her mouth. "Dick, I don't know about good guys and bad guys. I don't have time to think about that, and I'm just too tired. Still, you make me smile. By the way, I think you taught that lout a lesson."

I asked Mark what a "lout" was. He didn't know.

The police chief walked from his cruiser to my parents, who were standing together on the bridge. He was a good-sized man and breathing hard. He nodded to my mother and said, "Hello, Dick. I'm sorry we have to meet under these circumstances."

"Hello, Chief. I hope your brother is all right."

"He's fine."

"I'm sorry I knocked him out, but he was misbehaving."

"Let me talk to my officer."

The police chief then led the officer away from the bridge and next to my hiding place.

He quietly told the officer, "Look, you've got to release him. My brother was drinking and I'm sure he was in the wrong."

"Yeah, but I don't think it was self-defense, and that guy really laid him out."

The police chief slowly turned his head and looked toward where Mark and I were hiding. Then he paused, and looked over to my father. He continued talking to the officer, "You know who you just cuffed?"

"No."

"That's Dick Wales. He's just some college teacher now, but he was a big ass hero in the war. I'm sure my brother deserved what he got." The chief paused, and the deputy opened his mouth to speak. The chief put his hand on the deputy's shoulder and continued, "Look, I don't want some headline about arresting a decorated veteran who punched the chief's drunken brother. Do me a favor and release him."

"Chief," the officer attempted to whisper, "I am so sick and tired of these veterans getting…" The Chief put up his hand and interrupted, "I promise I'll make it up to you." He walked toward his cruiser and motioned to his brother to get into the passenger seat.

As the police cars headed away, my mother turned to my father, "Dear, it looks like you won't escape to the slammer today. But, Dick, let's steer clear of the police for a while."

My father nodded, "Good idea." He hugged my mother and gave her a kiss on the lips. She shook her head, laughed, and wriggled away. Then, he rubbed his hands together loudly, the same way he did on Sunday mornings while listening to Judy Garland, and turned toward the bush, "Boys, the coast is clear. You can come out now. We're all going to lay low for a while."

Chapter Two: *Summer Idyll*

Strapping the .22 rifle onto a thirteen-foot catamaran was tricky. There just wasn't much room left after the sleeping bags, water, and food were loaded onto the tight canvas platform and tied down with bungee cords and line. Finally, Mark, Alex, and I decided to strap the rifle onto the frame and sit on it when we needed to tack. Finished with preparations, we rolled the catamaran down the ramp on a homemade dolly. It was high tide in the harbor. We ditched the dolly on the rocks, jumped aboard, raised the mainsail and headed toward the jetties.

Our destination was Sandy Point, the tip of a long, undeveloped beach and wildlife refuge. To get there we simply needed to sail the eight-mile length of the barrier island, but first we had to survive the jetties and the mouth of the Merrimack River. The north and south jetties channel the powerful river into the Gulf of Maine. Emphasis on powerful. The current swirls, whirlpools, and crests into four-foot standing waves. And that's on a calm day without big boat traffic.

Today was not calm. A stiff east breeze was blowing onto shore as the tide turned and began to pump out into the Gulf. Whitecaps filled the troughs of the standing waves, which began to crest and break. And, there were plenty of large boats running through the jetties. Being fifteen and indestructible, Mark and I thought little about sailing a thirteen-foot boat through the maelstrom. Being thirteen and more thoughtful, Alex expressed his fears: "Hey guys, should we turn around?"

Mark, the only one of us with real sailing experience, laughed. "We can't turn around now or we'd be swamped." The little catamaran tacked up the next rolling wave and shuddered. Then we slid down the back of the wave and pitched violently up onto the next one.

Having sailed through the jetties before, I considered myself an old salt and needed to show my loyalty, "Yeah, Alex, Mark's right. We have to keep going forward."

The skipper of a lobster boat shook his head, smiled, and saluted as he steamed past us toward the harbor. Mark, at the helm, waved back.

Mark and I both yelled "Yeeehaaah" as we crested the next wave. We ducked, came about, and nearly cut off a large, orange powerboat churning into the harbor. The man behind the powerboat's steering wheel shouted something and gave us the finger. I yelled, "Hey, dickface, we have the right of way!" Mark laughed and shot up his middle finger.

The huge wake of a party boat slammed into the side of our small craft, nearly capsizing us. Alex screamed and then, to hide his panic, added a loud "Fuck this shit." Sitting on the downwind side of the tarpaulin, across from Mark and me, Alex began to pitch toward the water as a gust of wind filled the sail. He tried to clamp his hands onto the aluminum rail but grabbed the strapped-on rifle, with one hand on the barrel and the other near the stock. Above the sound of the breaking waves, the creaking sail, the banging stays, and the chugging motors, the clear explosion of a gunshot was unmistakable. Alex immediately raised his hands over his head, lost his balance, and pitched into the water.

Mark, remarkably calm, announced "I'll luff the sail, you grab him." I scrambled across the trampoline-like deck and looked down at the terrified Alex clinging to the port gunnel. "Would you like to come aboard?" Alex didn't answer, but Mark laughed. I reached under Alex's armpits and hauled him onto the tarpaulin. He laid

12

face up, breathing hard like a captured fish. Mark caught the wind in the sail and I hung on to Alex with one hand while grabbing the starboard railing with the other.

I looked at Mark, who shook his head and said, "Holy shit." I responded, "Maybe you should unload the .22 next time we sail."

"I had no idea. I should have checked it before we left. Alex, did you see where the bullet went?"

Alex looked up, but only said, "I think we should head back." Looking at Alex always gave me a bit of a shock because he looked a lot like me. Same wide face, sandy hair, blue eyes, and straight, broad nose. I suppose it should not have surprised me; after all, he was a second cousin once removed, or something like that. But it disturbed me because I didn't want him to look like me. First, he sometimes mildly smelled of mildew; the odor must have come from his summer house which always held a strong decaying smell when first opened. Second, his hair was always full of twigs, inch worms, and who knows what else. Third, he had the peculiar habit of bulging out his eyes when he was puzzled or annoyed. He was doing the eye-bulging thing right now. Fourth, even though he was warm and kind, he sometimes could rub us the wrong way. He liked to brag about his parents' money, how his father was a big deal in the oil industry, and how his grandmother had some big house in some fancy town on Long Island. Mark and I doubted all this crap because his father was never around and we hardly ever saw his mother. When asked, Alex explained her absence by saying she had a headache or was off at some fancy party.

Each summer Alex would show up for a month with his mother and live in the nearby dilapidated summer house that was owned by his extended family. Almost immediately, he would hunt us down. He seemed to be a constant presence for that one month.

Several times a week he would show up at our door at dinner time and claim that his mother was sleeping or away. My parents always warmly invited him in, and my father would quickly set an extra place next to the head of the table. With Alex sitting next to my father, I became more and more irritated as my father peppered Alex with questions and laughed at his stories. Sometimes my father would look my way during these dinners, and I might roll my eyes at one of Alex's exaggerations, only to get a stern parental look in return. After Alex left one night, my father asked me why I seemed upset with the younger boy. I explained that I did not like his bragging about money and found many of his stories to be ridiculous. That was a true answer, but hardly complete. It didn't take much to figure out that I was jealous and would have loved to be sitting next to my father instead of between two younger sisters who fought often during meals. My father gave a sphinxlike, and completely unsatisfying, response, "Money is not the only wealth, and you are much wealthier than Alex in so many ways."

Truth be told, Mark and I mostly looked forward to Alex's summer arrival. After all, things got boring in the country and a new face, even one looking like my own, was welcome. The three of us would fish, and Mark and I would often steal his new fishing lures when Alex wasn't looking. Once, after Mark had secretly pocketed a brand-new Jitterbug, Alex hauled up a fat twenty-inch pickerel, a true trophy from the small mill pond. Mark and I, dumbfounded and jealous, promptly lied and assured Alex that we also caught pickerel of equal or greater size with regularity. Then, I looked about Alex's open tackle box for something else to steal. Perhaps, our actions sometimes bordered upon the uncaring or cruel, but we just didn't think about it in those terms. We genuinely liked Alex; we equally liked having someone lower on the totem pole.

So, we were left to ramble with Alex and, occasionally, assert our dominance, particularly if our parents were not around. And, being the early to mid-1960s, our parents were rarely around. They were busy raising younger children or making a living. Call it the benign neglect of independent and adventurous boys in the country, but it all seemed to work. At least when firearms, secretly borrowed from the gun rack of Mark's dad, were not in hand.

We tacked again, slid past the end of the south jetty, where at last it was calm. Out on the ocean, away from the churning river mouth, only long swells headed toward shore, causing the bell buoy to clang and, farther out, the "whistler" to give its slow, mournful sound. We were free. Then we heard the siren. The three of us looked back at the river mouth and saw the Coast Guard rescue boat, lights flashing and siren sounding. It was stopped next to the orange power boat, but we could see little else.

Mark, usually unflappable in a boat, nervously said, "We better hide the .22. Someone must have heard the shot and called the Coast Guard." He took a breath, smiled, and added, "Alex, your fingerprints must be on the trigger. It looks like you could go to prison. So, change of plans, just keep the .22 where it is." I laughed. I always was amazed how quickly Mark could think through a situation.

Then, we watched the Coast Guard leave the orange boat and race toward the lobster boat, which was well into the harbor. We cheered and sailed south, away from the jetties and the Coast Guard. Later, I read the report in the town's newspaper. The powerboat driver heard a shot and noticed a bullet hole in his hull near the waterline. He immediately called the Coast Guard and reported that he had squabbled with the lobster boat skipper earlier that day. Lobster men were well known for being armed, so the Coast Guard stopped the lobster boat at its mooring, boarded, and searched. They found no rifle, only a shotgun that had not been fired recently. The Coast Guard listed the incident as "unsolved," while the paper quoted the power boat driver as angrily complaining that the Coast Guard was "inept and incompetent."

But, at the time, we only knew that we were free, sailing in the sunshine over the green ocean. Mark and I leaned back on bent elbows and watched the nearly empty beach slip past. The gentle rocking of the swells was nearly hypnotic.

Alex crawled to the edge of the canvas. "Where are you going Alex, taking another swim?"

"I think I'm going to be sick." And, sure enough, he was.

Mark adjusted the tiller slightly; his brown eyes gleamed as he said, "Well, we went by boat, but it looks like Alex is going by rail."

Alex, wiping his mouth and bugging out his eyes, responded, "Shut up, I don't feel that good. Can't you sail this boat more smoothly?"

Mark and I laughed and looked down the beach toward the Sandy Point.

I took over the helm and we cruised along. Alex leaned over the rail until we surfed the catamaran up onto the beach. The Point was beautiful. Terns dove into the clear water and black-backed gulls strutted possessively along the shore.

Alex jumped onto the sand and was a new man. "Finally! Let me help unload the boat. Where is my food bag?"

Immediately, Mark and I went swimming. The cool water seemed to swallow us as we dove down to harass the prehistoric horseshoe crabs that slowly traversed the sandy bottom.

SUMMER IDYLL

"Come swim, Alex!" Mark yelled. "No thanks," he replied. "I can't swim as well as you two guys." Instead, Alex rolled out his sleeping bag on the sand, sat on it with his food bag in his lap, and ate.

After swimming Mark and I strolled around the Point toward a mucky portion that looked good for clams. We watched for bubbles coming from the mud and, then, using our hands, we dug furiously and captured the large, thin shelled clams. Taking our time, we collected at least three dozen steamers.

"These will taste great, Mark."

"Did you bring some butter?"

"Yeah," I responded, "plenty."

Stretching our T-shirts as baskets, we carried the dripping treasure back around the Point. I looked ahead and saw Alex standing by his sleeping bag while three larger boys surrounded him. The largest of these strangers was pushing Alex in the chest, and Alex plainly was crying.

Without any thought, I dropped my clams and sprinted toward the group. The boys were focused on Alex and did not notice me. I launched myself and, using my shoulder, tackled the boy pushing Alex and drove him into the sand. Seeing that I had knocked the wind out of him, I sprang up and grabbed the next boy and placed him into a headlock and twisted hard.

By his wheezes and cries, I knew I was hurting the boy, but this thought did not seem to make much difference. I twisted harder, and told him to take his friends and leave. By then the first boy had regained his feet, and he and the third boy were approaching me. My fury evaporating, I recognized that the approaching boys, both about my size, were not in a negotiating mood. I knew Alex would not be much help in the upcoming fight and decided to throw the second boy to the ground and face the two who were approaching with clenched fists.

"Can I help you boys?" It was Mark, and he was easily walking toward us with the rifle casually swinging at his side. The three boys turned, looked at Mark, and ran to their skiff. We slowly followed them and laughed as they frantically pulled the rope to start their outboard. The engine finally coughed to a start, and they sped across the bay.

"The rifle is not loaded, but I don't think they'll be back soon," Mark observed.

Alex, rather formally, approached both of us and shook our hands, repeating, "Thank you so much for saving me."

"Hey, Alex," I said, "it's no big thing. No one gets to mess with my friend."

Alex practically beamed. "You see," Mark added, "Rich here is the brawn and I'm the brains. Nothing comes between the three musketeers."

"What's a musketeer?" Alex asked.

Mark replied, "They didn't teach that stuff at your fancy school? Well, it means that we are like brothers." Alex's eyes began to fill, and he looked away. Mark and I headed back to collect the clams.

The sun began to slant slightly toward evening, and I suggested that we begin preparations for dinner.

"Those kids threw most of my food to the gulls," Alex said glumly.

"Don't worry. We have plenty of steamers and can get more."

Alex's eyes bugged out, "I don't know if I like steamers. Can I have some of your food?"

Mark explained, "We didn't bring much for dinner because we knew we could dig steamers. Try one and see if you like it."

"O.K., I'll try one," Alex said, "but, if I don't like it, what did you bring for breakfast? Can I have some of that? I'm starving." The kid was persistent.

I countered, "We just brought instant oatmeal, but we can cook that up. I brought a chocolate bar, what about that?"

"Sure," he replied, defeated.

Alex ripped into the candy bar and finished it before we set the fire.

The steamers were delicious, and Alex bravely swallowed two of them before I cooked up three packets of instant oatmeal which he devoured quickly.

As the fire died down, twilight came with thousands of swallows swooping in the air. The three of us lay on the catamaran deck and returned to the .22.

Alex interrupted the mood, "Do you think we should be doing this? After all," he added in an annoying tone, "this *is* a wildlife refuge."

"Shut up!" we bellowed in unison and began firing. At first, we picked out a particular swallow and aimed. But, since their swooping flight was so jerky and unpredictable, Mark and I hit nothing. Alex was roused by our lack of success and demanded, "Let me see the gun." He began to blaze away wildly with no greater success. Eventually the box of shells was empty.

It was dark. Mark pointed to the lights across the sound and said, "You know, that's Ipswich, and we know those girls who live there."

Alex closely guarded against any aggrandizement in Mark's or my prestige. "Oh, sure you know some girls. Where did you meet them? I bet you're lying, or they are first-class dogs."

Mark paused, assuming a professorial air, "Actually, Alex, we met these two girls at a private school mixer in April. They are both pretty, and I believe Rich asked one to the formal dance."

"Did she go?"

I interrupted, "She was busy with some test."

"Hah, I knew it! Swing batter, batter, STRIIIKE!"

Mark laughed, "Alex, be gentle with Rich's delicate feelings. He did give you the chocolate."

"That chocolate bar was small."

"Good point, Alex," I conceded. "But we are going to take the catamaran over to the Ipswich pavilion and look for those two girls."

"In the dark? Without any wind?"

"Sure, we'll paddle. It's going to be slack tide soon. Come along. I bet there are plenty of girls. I'll buy you an ice cream cone."

Alex hesitated and softly asked, "What if those three guys are over there?"

With unthinking bravado, I assured Alex that we would all beat the shit out of them if we saw those three losers.

"Do you promise to buy me that ice cream cone?"

I replied, "I promise."

SUMMER IDYLL

We all agreed that paddling the small catamaran was torture. Finally, we scraped up onto Pavilion Beach and headed to the brightly lit Pavilion. There were girls, many in groups or with clinging boyfriends. Why I thought I would meet a dance date from three months ago was a mystery. I slowly walked around the structure trying to look cool while looking for my former date. No luck. Mark, with his almost platinum blond hair, fine features, and deep tan was much better at this type of thing than I was. He soon had a group of girls talking to him. I decided to get an ice cream cone and looked for Alex. I couldn't find him. He wasn't near Mark and wasn't anywhere in the Pavilion. I looked around the perimeter of the structure in expanding circles, but no Alex. I jogged down to the ice cream parlor to see if Alex was there. No luck.

I jogged back and waved to Mark. He broke away from the girls and asked, "Did you find that girl?"

I wanted to tell him about Alex's absence, but first answered his question, "No, no luck. How 'bout you?"

"I got a girl's phone number, and we might go out."

I wasn't surprised. With his looks and quick wit, Mark was really good with girls. I turned and smiled, "Hey, Mark, that's great!"

"I guess so. It's no big thing." At fifteen years old, I thought getting a girl's number was a really big thing.

Mark put his arm over my shoulder. This was unusual. He was never a touchy, feely guy. "I'm sorry you didn't find your date. I remember her. She was pretty and seemed interested in you. Well, it's her loss. We better hurry before the tide picks up."

I blurted out that I had lost Alex.

Mark turned toward me, "How could you lose him? He just wanted an ice cream cone." I explained that I had last seen him hanging around some older girls, and, then, I couldn't find him anywhere. We decided to search the beach below the lighted Pavilion. After ten minutes, we still hadn't found him, and I was nervous.

I reminded Mark, "Our parents will kill us if we lost Alex." Mark nodded, and we headed toward some dinghies stored upside down along the beach. Still no Alex. We jogged toward some large smooth rocks farther along the shore. At first, I couldn't see him. Then, I saw a body laying very still on the largest rock.

He was not alone. A girl with long blonde hair lay beside him on her side and was leaning over and kissing him. I nudged Mark and pointed.

"Jesus Christ," Mark whispered. We silently stared. Then the girl moved and lay right on top of Alex. "I wonder if she knows he's only thirteen," I whispered back to Mark.

We continued staring and, although the moonlight didn't show much, it appeared that Alex was working his hand under her shirt. "Do you think we should rescue him?," I asked. Mark stifled a laugh, "he sure doesn't need our help now." Finally, we decided that the tide would really begin to rip soon. So, we backed away and called out to Alex while pretending to search for him.

"I'll be right there," he replied with hoarse voice. The sound of his voice carried clearly in the still night air.

"Who is that?" the girl asked. She seemed to have an accent.

"Oh, they're just my brothers."

"Well," the girl continued, "call me next Saturday if you are around." Yes, definitely an accent.

SUMMER IDYLL

I stared at Mark and hissed "I think she's European or something!" Mark grinned, shook his head, and whispered, "Well, little Alex and a Scandinavian blonde. Wonders never cease." Alex came jogging toward us with a huge grin.

The tide was picking up, but we made it back to Sandy Point straining at our paddles and talking about Alex's adventure.

Once ashore, Alex insisted on climbing into his crumpled sleeping bag on the beach and soon was softly snoring. Probably, I thought, dreaming about that blonde.

Mark and I lay upon the tight tarpaulin deck in our sleeping bags and looked at the stars. In soft voices, we replayed a familiar topic: "Can you imagine being the first settlers to come to this land? All the fish and birds that would have been here? No towns or buildings."

Still staring at the stars, Mark replied, "it would have been beautiful." Then he turned his head to face me and smile, "we probably still wouldn't have been able to hit anything with a rifle or flintlock or whatever they used."

Mark swatted at a mosquito and continued, "I want to live in the Alaskan wilderness or be a cowboy on some big ranch in the Rocky Mountains, someplace where there is still big game and no mosquitoes."

I reminded him that this latter thought was silly because he was allergic to horses and cows. "Hey," he responded, "it's a dream, and I'm still working out the details."

We both laughed softly and listened to the river lapping on the sand and the Atlantic waves hitting the shore around the Point. Soon, we drifted off to sleep.

Alex's scream woke us. He was frantically thrashing in his sleeping bag and saying nonsensical things. "Shut off the light! I don't want to be here! Get off!"

We both ran over to him and helped him get into a sitting position.

"Whoa there Alex," Mark began. "It's all right."

I continued, "You're just having a bad dream. Alex, Alex, open your eyes, it was just a dream."

Alex's eyes opened with their familiar bulge. He looked at me, then he grabbed me around the shoulders, hugging me with all his strength. "I'm sorry, I'm sorry."

"Hey, no reason to be sorry. Just a bad dream. Come over with us, and lay down on top of the boat."

Without a word, Alex struggled out of his bag and, clad in his underwear, trudged over to the catamaran while scratching at his insect bites.

Mark and I let him have the middle position on the tarpaulin.

"Hey Alex, don't you want to get your sleeping bag?"

"No, it's full of bugs. I'll be fine."

I knew he wouldn't be. I unzipped my bag and spread it over both of us.

Mark asked, "Hey, what was your dream about? That blond girl?"

"No, not at all. You wouldn't want to know, and I don't want to talk about it."

I gave Alex my sweatshirt to roll up as a pillow and asked, "Do you have bad dreams often?"

"Yeah, I think so. It's sort of the same one over and over. I don't want to talk about it." Alex's voice cracked when he added, "Anyway, you wouldn't believe it. I'm tired." With that, Alex rolled over onto his stomach and closed his eyes. Mark and I looked at each other and shrugged.

I lay on my back, looking at the stars and wondering about Alex's bad dream. Alex began to snore. Then, he rolled onto his side, close to me, and placed his open palm on the middle of my chest. At first, I was surprised, but its warmth felt good and Alex was breathing calmly. Alex usually wasn't calm, and I didn't want to wake him.

I woke when the sun began to rise from the ocean. The light was almost blinding. Mark nudged me and said in a sleepy voice, "What is Alex dragging?"

I looked over and saw Alex's silhouetted figure dragging something toward us along the beach. When he came closer, I noticed that his head was down and he was straining as he dragged a tangle of rope, wood and metal. He lifted his head, saw us, and yelled, "It's a lobster trap, and there are lobsters in it. I just can't open it."

We hopped down from the boat, and Mark replied, "Alex, there's a law against taking someone's lobster trap. You know, this *is* a wildlife refuge."

Alex laughed and shouted, "Ah, shut up!"

Mark and I laughed in reply and ran to Alex. We cut some of the line, then smashed in the trap door enough to take out four good-sized lobsters.

We started the fire, let the driftwood burn to coals, stabbed each lobster through the brain, placed them on the coals, and covered them with seaweed. After a while, we turned them over and roasted the other side.

Lobster juice and butter ran off our chins onto our bare chests as we cracked the shells and devoured the meat. We decided that Alex, having found the trap in the tide pool rocks and being the faster eater, should have the fourth lobster.

Alex then announced, "Let's strip down and clean off with a swim." Mark and I answered by quickly shedding our shorts and hitting the water with Alex close behind. The water was stunningly cold. As Mark and I plodded toward shore, Alex ran up between us and placed his arms over both our shoulders. We responded by draping our arms over his shoulders. He gripped us harder. With our shins still covered by water, Alex turned the three of us toward the quickly rising sun. Although he was out of breath, he managed to say, "Isn't this beautiful? Isn't this just great?

"

Chapter Three: *Marseille*

There is something undeniably erotic about watching your college girlfriend, her cheeks flushed and her unbound breasts stretching the fabric of her worn T-shirt, drag a small Tunisian man along a train station floor while clutching her leather satchel strap that had somehow lodged itself around the poor man's neck. The diminutive, dark man had tried to steal the satchel but had not anticipated Alex's quickness and strength. After he ran past us and grabbed the satchel, Alex, a small, pretty, Quaker girl from the Philadelphia suburbs, had reared back on the leather strap as if setting the hook on a marlin. The result was that the little Tunisian man, his forward motion suddenly halted, left his feet and hit the tile floor hard. Alex then hauled in her catch while I admired her with a stiffening erection.

Alex and I had met in the late 1960s, on one of those rare warm days when spring breaks out on upstate New York campuses after months of miserable weather. Speakers were placed in windows, the Grateful Dead and Joplin blast forth, Frisbees fly, students sprawl on any patch of sundrenched grass, and the males thank God for their high draft numbers. I was drinking a bock beer and reading a freshman history textbook when she shyly asked if I had taken notes in the class she missed. As I squinted into the sun at this redhead with green eyes and freckles, dressed in a short denim skirt and a loose peasant top, I was captured.

For the next three years we spent hours talking, riding bikes, taking study breaks, and making love. On the subject of lovemaking, Alex had substantially more experience than I. Thank God. I was in dire need of direction, encouragement, and confidence in this arena. And what better time to learn about the joys of romance than the late '60s? AIDS was unknown, birth control pills were easily obtained, and condoms frequently were deemed unnecessary. In Alex's bed I learned a truth that I never would have believed during my all-male high school years; if approached with just a dollop of sensitivity and civility, young women enjoyed sex just as much as young men. This was an astounding discovery.

There are few things as intense as that first serious sexual relationship. Learning the details of the female body was like experiencing one's first total solar eclipse: mesmerizing and very satisfying. Friends were jealous of our relationship, and I felt lucky. By senior year we somehow ended up together in a large dormitory room with two beds pushed together to form a massive mattress. Cheap Indian fabrics were stitched together and hung as a canopy surrounding the bed. With wall posters, candles, and Crosby, Stills, Nash & Young, we engaged in increasingly adventurous sex. My male friends, outside of Alex's hearing, called the room the "pleasure palace." We were the campus couple; then again, it was a small campus.

After graduation, we took the then common route of liberal arts majors. We bought backpacks and Eurail passes and headed to Great Britain and the continent. We had enough money, barely, to prevent growing up for at least six more months. While Nixon connived and the Viet Nam War raged, we spent hours at the Tate Gallery, the Louvre, and Chartres. Alex would softly lecture on a famous stained-glass window or the way in which Rembrandt and Vermeer used light. We both loved the travel, the sights, and the unstructured days. There were plenty of times, however, when Alex would stare intently at one of the seemingly endless statutes of Mary or a painting of yet another odd-looking baby Jesus, and my mind would drift to Fenway Park, or netting crabs for dinner from a salt water pond, or another similarly profane image of

28

MARSEILLE

Americana. Once, sitting in a French park with fresh bread, a fine local cheese, and a bottle of rough red wine, Alex asked me what else I wanted to do. Lying on my back, I replied: "Nothing. I just want to feel the sun, watch the clouds, and look at those weird bushes that the French spend hours trimming so that they don't look like bushes." Alex laughed and said that that the bushes were called "topiary" and added, "Sometimes I think you lack all culture." "Perhaps," I replied with a smile, "but, please, let's avoid any more fifteenth century Romanesque churches. If I have to walk through another, I may die of boredom."

"No problem," she responded with a smile, "there is a charming chapel two blocks from here with amazing Gothic architecture. And, lucky for you, it was built in the seventeenth century."

I groaned loudly and asked, "Could you hand me another hunk of that good bread?"

"Only if you get up and move toward that chapel. It gets three stars in the Michelin guide." I groaned again and slowly rose.

We rented a run down, third floor room on the Left Bank of Paris, complete with aging frescos and a shaky balcony. I walked out onto the balcony and told Alex to come and see the stunning view. "In a bit, I am studying this fresco. I think it shows the allegory of Hagar and Sarah." I did not respond, but shook my head and gazed at the expanse of roofs and picturesque streets. I wondered, who the hell are Hagar and Sarah? But I knew that such a question voiced to Alex would display my cultural ignorance and, after all, I really wasn't interested in the answer.

Later that evening, we strolled back from a café arm in arm to our abode. Alex always was quick to take my arm and snuggle to my side as we walked, particularly after a couple of glasses of wine. My anticipation was running high as we passed the Sorbonne under antique lamplight. Then Alex said, "I've been thinking. You're my best friend. I hope you know that. Still, I just think that we are so different. It becomes clearer each day."

"Well," I responded lightly, trying to avoid her serious tone, "opposites attract."

She replied, "They may not attract forever. I just don't know if we have a future."

"Oh, come on," I scoffed, "just because you enjoy staring at some Roman marble stud while I like looking at the breasts of Botticelli's Venus?" The wine helped with the next statement, "What do you want, a dilettante talking breathlessly about some Gothic arch?"

"I think you've had too much wine."

"Or," I said flatly, "not enough." At the time, I thought such a brittle response made me sound witty and sophisticated. Alex usually ignored such comments. She probably realized that I was attempting to build a protective and worldly façade to hide the fact that I remained a relatively innocent, straight forward, and sometimes naïve boy.

But, at the time, all I knew was that my sexual anticipation had fled, replaced with an empty knot of irritation bordering upon bitterness.

After walking a block in silence, she asked, "Rich, are you angry with me? Why don't we talk?"

God, I thought to myself, she always wants to talk. I knew that I would botch up any conversation about our differences. I just wanted to stride along silently and angrily and feel sorry for myself. But such male brooding would hurt her, and I never wanted to hurt her. So, I answered, "I was just thinking of an old friend.

30

MARSEILLE

Did I ever tell you I had a friend growing up who was also named Alex?"

"No. What was she like?"

"It was a boy. His name was Alexander, not Alexandra. He was great but, at times, he could be a bit irritating and frustrating."

She pulled my arm closer, hard against the side of her breast, and laughed, "Are you implying that I am irritating?" She didn't wait for a reply, but turned, grabbed my shoulders and looked up into my face: "You truly are so important to me. I love being with you. But, after this trip, I think we might each go our own way. I never want to hurt you. You know you own a piece of my heart. I'm just trying to be honest and open." Then she gave me a soft, lingering kiss.

My initial reaction to the kiss focused on one thought: make-up sex underneath the fading frescos. The pleasure palace returns! The anticipation was back. It took a conscious effort to think beyond this promising possibility.

The problem was that I also loved being with her, despite her honesty and clear judgment. I knew she probably was right, but I wanted to take the cowardly approach and have a good time while ignoring the matter. Upon return to the States, she planned to look for an internship at some Philadelphia museum while I was thinking vaguely about law school. In typical fashion, I had not given a single thought to what that separation might do to our relationship. If forced to think ahead, I simply would have assumed continuation as a couple even if I often dreamed of streams and forests while she focused on art and literature. Frankly, however, I didn't spend much, if any, time thinking about the future; it was all carpe diem for this guy. I can still see her concerned expression as she searched my eyes under the lamplight. I have never returned to Paris.

Eventually the colder weather forced us south toward Spain. The train to Barcelona was beset by engine failures and striking railroad workers. After many stops and starts, we were shifted to an ancient train with an elegant first-class coach and several rail cars with rudimentary wooden benches. Our Eurail passes put Alex and me on the benches along with a few hardy farmers of southern France, some crated chickens, and many migrants from northern Africa. A second rail strike left us stranded at the imposing Marseille train station close to midnight. It was when exiting the third-class car and walking into the station that one of our fellow travelers attempted the theft.

Alex hugged me after she had rescued her satchel, and the Tunisian slipped groggily away. "I am so glad you're here," she breathed into my shirt. She clung to me for a long time. When her breathing slowed, I praised her bravery.

She tried to make light of it, "Not bad for a pacifist."

"Not bad at all."

We turned to watch a group of nuns in black habits and white pointed hats disembark from the elegant coach and file into the first-class waiting room. A large nun, apparently the mother superior, was leading the column, speaking rapid French, and clearing a path through the mostly Algerian and Tunisian passengers milling about the station. She pulled open the impressive glass and wood door to the waiting room and held it open for her charges. As the column disappeared into the room, she pointed at us, spoke in French, and gestured that we were to join the nuns. Despite her godly mission, she may have slipped to the racist conclusion that Alex and I, being among the few whites in the midnight station, other than her sisters, were also first-class passengers. I did not hesitate and did not correct her misassumption. Instead, I quickly directed Alex into the large waiting room, which held a huge upholstered circular couch at its center. The nuns were sitting on the couch, with a few lying diagonally with her head in the lap of a neighboring nun.

One nun smiled at us and invited us to sit beside her. The mother superior then ascended to the large oval raised center of the couch, sat down with legs crossed, and, from that elevated perch, surveyed her flock. When two small black men cracked open the heavy door and attempted to enter, the mother superior yelled at them and directed two nuns to stand guard at the door. Given the superior's imposing size and voice, or her moral position, the two men fled. The waiting room assumed an almost surreal quiet as the two door guards shooed away other dark intruders, and the mother superior smiled down upon her white charges. Being a child of the sixties, I recognized the racial overtones of the situation, but I was tired and safe, and I sure wasn't going challenge the big nun.

Alex and I spoke quietly about the long day, but I began to nod off.

"You are so tired. You're falling asleep talking to me. Here, lie down."

She pulled one of my shoulders and positioned me like some of the nuns, with my head in her lap and my legs folded on the circular couch. Even overcome with tiredness, my head being nestled next to her crotch provided a familiar jolt. Then, she slowly and softly stroked my hair and forehead. It felt heavenly.

Alex, whose fluency contrasted with my lingual ignorance, said something in French to the mother superior who responded, "Ah, oui, merci." Alex, who knew I loved her high sweet voice, began to sing. Her fingers continued to ruffle my hair as she sang the Lerner and Loewe tune from Camelot, "If Ever I Would Leave You." As her beautiful voice filled the high-ceilinged room, I drifted off to sleep. I must have known, in some subconscious region, that Alex was correct and that we would part forever after this trip, for I dreamt of being in a light-filled forest. I was alone, completely free, and distinctly happy. Then my dream shifted abruptly, as only dreams do, and my father stood like a fortress and greeted me with a strong hug and kiss on the cheek while my mother smiled at his side and waited to embrace me.

Chapter Four: *The Running Dog*

How did I get here?

You mean in this holding cell? Well, it's all because of the damn Running Dog.

There I was in the Three Forks area. Actually, I was fishing the Ruby and borrowing my friend's car. I drove it up from West and saw this sweet stretch of water. You know, riffles running into clear pools and those nice gentle bends where the trout like to hang out. I practically ran off the road when I saw the river. A hop, skip, and a jump and I was over that barbed wire fence and wet wading in Big Sky country. Beautiful! All you needed was a hopper tied onto 5X and a well-placed cast. It sure beat that Eastern fishing where you crawl around the alders with black flies in your eyes and up your nose and try to catch those little brookies.

Well there I was catching chunky browns and rainbows when some sheriff's car pulled over, and this sheriff got out. He was all dressed in his uniform and wearing this Stetson, and he hopped over the fence and yelled over to me.

"You know you're trespassing, don't you?"

Now, I know my rights and I'm not letting any tin star interfere with my fishing. So, I told him that I was not trespassing and let him know about the Montana Stream Access Law. That law says that I can wade in any navigable waterway. The Ruby is small, but it's navigable. To reinforce my argument, I added that I was a lawyer. I had just completed law school and passed the bar.

When I informed the sheriff of my being a member of the Massachusetts bar, he appeared less than impressed. He said flatly, "I know the law. But you have to get to the stream from a public access. There's no public access to this stream for miles. This is

Adolf Krupp's land and he gets real agitated with trespassers. That's why there are all these signs. You're lucky I spotted you. You don't want no trouble with Krupp's men."

Given this new information and the short shrift he gave to my legal education, I was glad I didn't mention that I was taking the summer off before starting a prestigious clerkship with a federal judge. Instead, I slowly waded out of that sweet stretch. The idea of Krupp's henchmen was a little scary. I knew it was too good to be true. The fishing had been so fine, almost easy. That Krupp sure is a lucky man.

The sheriff introduced himself. I'll say this: he was polite. "T.J. Pettibone. Deputy Sheriff, Beaverhead County. Most folks call me T.J. That your car parked over on the side of the road?"

I admitted that the old yellow Ford Fiesta was mine and headed over to it. T.J. walked with me and apologized for ruining my fishing. He was beginning to seem like a nice guy.

I threw my vest and rod into the backseat and got into the car. Then I turned the screwdriver. You see, my friend lost the key a long time ago, and we always used a screwdriver in the ignition. It worked fine.

Then I heard the sheriff say, "Whoa there, cowboy. What's with the screwdriver?"

I told him the whole story about my friend and losing the key a long time ago.

"But I thought you said the car was yours."

I explained about how I borrowed the car from my friend down in West. And, no I can't find the registration; there was so much junk in the glove box, I couldn't find anything. But I know it's his

36

car. He's had it for a couple of years and, no, I didn't realize that the license plates didn't match the car. How would I know?

He asked me for my friend's name, and I gave it to him. Then, he wanted his address, and I was honest with him. I told the sheriff that he doesn't have just one address. My friend camps out a lot down in West and sleeps over at a bunch of friends' houses. The Deputy Sheriff began looking all around and, then, asked me to step out of the car.

"Sorry, but I can't let you drive an unregistered vehicle. I'll give you a ride into town, so why don't you get your gear while I call this in."

What was I supposed to do? I gathered my vest, rod, tent and sleeping bag and headed over to the cruiser. The sheriff held his finger up for me to wait while he talked on his walky-talky thing. Eventually he let me into the back of the cruiser.

"Sorry about that. Just running a record. We'll just have to check out a few things when we get to the station. They're going to have to tow that vehicle. Your friend can pick it up when he shows his license and registration, and he better bring a proof of purchase." T.J. Pettibone looked at me in the rearview mirror, "A bill of sale for that car, understand?"

I nodded. At this point, I wasn't feeling too kind toward the world. I went from casting dries for eager trout to sitting in the back of a cruiser. The day sure went to shit fast. As we left that Ford Fiesta beside that gravel road, I felt a little guilty. But I told myself that it was a crappy car anyway, and my friend was a little sketchy sometimes. Maybe leaving that car in Beaverhead County wasn't such a bad idea.

So, I sat around the "Beaverhead County Law Enforcement Center." What a joke. It's an office in a rundown building with a couple of deputies looking at computer screens. It's right next door to the "Weed Supervisor for the Beaverhead." And there I was feeling uncomfortable in my wet pants, socks, and wading shoes and lugging around my rod, vest, and sleeping bag. I must have left the tent back near the Fiesta. Finally, one of the overweight deputies looked up from the computer screen and said, "You're free to go, no active warrants or defaults."

Of course, there weren't any warrants or defaults! But where was I supposed to go? They wouldn't let me drive the Ford Fiesta.

"You can catch the bus in front of the café. It will come through tomorrow morning. Take you up to Great Falls. From there you can go anywhere."

Tomorrow morning? Great Falls? Well, I told myself, maybe I can fish the Missouri up there. You know, get in below Holder Dam and wade that spring creek water. Sometimes, you just have to suck it up. So, after a few beers and a night on the hard ground of Dillon, I was waiting for the Greyhound heading north.

The bus pulled up, but it said "Missoula" on the front. Missoula? What happened to Great Falls and fishing the Missouri? Well, it seems that the Great Falls bus doesn't show up until the afternoon. I looked around and I saw Deputy Sheriff T.J. Pettibone sitting in his cruiser across the street watching me. That did it. I had enough of Dillon. It was time to leave. Anyway, there's the Clark's Fork up there in Missoula. Maybe I could catch a ride down to Lolo Creek or the Bitterroot. Up I stepped and handed the driver cash. He didn't like separating the still damp bills, but that's what sometimes happens when you go wet wading with your wallet. Anyway, he gave me the slow eye roll and looked down at my wading shoes. I must have left my sneakers back in the Fiesta, but at least the wading shoes had dried out enough so they didn't squish as I walked down the aisle.

I hadn't showered in a while. The Beaverhead County Park in Dillon didn't have any spa facilities. So, I thought I better look for an empty row of seats. The Running Dog was crowded and the only empty row was way in the back. I dozed off pretty quickly and didn't wake until we pulled into Deer Lodge.

There's not much to Deer Lodge except the prison. As you drive in off the highway, there's this bright red sign that says that the Chamber of Commerce welcomes you to historic Deer Lodge. Despite the sign, no one wanted to get off at Deer Lodge, and we just sat there. Eventually the door wheezed open and this big, tall Native American dude with a black pony-tail stepped onto the bus with this short girl. He looked around for a seat. Just my luck, the only two open seats together were across from me.

He started walking to the rear, and he looked scary, with a face that's all angles and raven-like eyes. "What the hell." he said in a voice like crunching stream gravel, "They're putting the Indians in the back of the bus like fucking Rosa Parks." Now I could tell that the two Grandma Moses-type women in front of me didn't like that type of language. The bus driver just shook his head and smiled. I was tempted to point out that technically Rosa Parks didn't sit in the back of the bus. That's why she's so famous. But, no one was messing with this big dude.

He and the girl settled in, and he immediately whipped out a green, square bottle and took a long pull. He handed it to the girl, who took a sip and made a face. I didn't blame her. It must have been Jägermeister. Have you ever tasted that crap? It would take the bark off a tree. He grabbed the bottle back and took another hit and then started making out with the girl. You never know who you're going to meet on the Running Dog.

They were both Indians; I guess I should call them Native Americans. But they looked almost like opposites. He was this hard, rough, tall guy and she small and pretty, with round cheeks and short black hair. She reminded me a little of the Sacagawea face on the gold dollar coin that I keep in my pocket for good luck.

I looked out the window as the bus lumbered up the entrance ramp of the highway. I could hear them going at it pretty hot and heavy, and I glanced over. He had his hands all over her. While he's nuzzling her neck, she caught me looking. And then she smiled at me! I immediately turned and started staring at the median strip like it was the most interesting thing since the moon landing.

Next thing I heard was his snoring. I turned back and she's gently pushing him off her and back into his seat. It didn't wake him. He's passed out with his head back, mouth open and the Jager bottle between his thighs.

"Typical Indian boy," she leaned toward me and whispered with a laugh, "a little action and he's gone. You'd think, after spending time at the pen, he'd be more interested."

How are you supposed to respond to that? Spending time in the maximum security prison at Deer Lodge! I knew this guy looked scary; what did he do to end up at Deer Lodge? And, what's the story with this Sacagawea-look-alike?

I just nodded and looked at the highway median. You never know who you're going to meet on the Running Dog.

After a few minutes, she leaned into the aisle and spoke again: "Hey little big man, have you ever had bathroom bo bo?"

THE RUNNING DOG

Bathroom bo bo? Could it mean what I thought? No, I must have misunderstood. After all, there was an innocence in her dark eyes, and her smile seemed so gentle. But then she lifted a foil packet from her bag that looked quite familiar, rose, straightened her short skirt, placed her other hand softly on my shoulder as if needing balance, and entered the small toilet right behind my row. She left the door ajar.

Talk about setting the hook.

I admit it; I was fidgeting in my seat. The older woman in front of me turned and stared right at me. Her cold, gray eyes glared, "Don't you dream of taking the bait and going in there with that girl!" Then I heard the girl clear her throat in the bathroom. The door was still ajar. I reasoned, hey, I'm twenty-three, single, and it's been a long time. After all, I argued with myself, she might need some sort of help. And, I repeated, it had been a long time. I looked at the sleeping Indian long and hard. He was still snoring, head back, mouth open. Now I noticed, through the gap in his windbreaker, that he had a gun stuck in a shoulder holster. A gun! Man, the laws out here are crazy. Here's a guy straight from Deer Lodge packing heat. This made me rethink the whole matter. Then, I got up and opened the door.

The bathroom was incredibly small, and she wasn't in the mood for waiting. First, she wanted one hundred bucks. When I said something witty like, "I didn't know this was a commercial transaction," she responded, "You think you're here because of your looks little big man?" I told her that I didn't have close to one hundred dollars. "Give me your wallet and let me see." What was I supposed to do? Especially with the big guy sleeping four feet away. She took the rest of my cash. "Why's it all wet?" I told her that it was a long story.

Now it's not easy to pull clothes down, slip things on, and do your job in that small a space—especially when you are thinking about a big freaking armed felon snoring on the other side of the paper-thin door. But I seemed to get the work done, all while still wearing the wading shoes.

Maybe I rushed things a little bit because the Indian girl didn't look all that happy when she sat back down in her seat. And maybe we were a little obvious because the two Grandma Moses passengers were sending us angry looks. The good news was that the boyfriend was still snoring. I went back to staring at that highway median strip.

The big guy woke pretty soon and the couple went back at it. Then she took him into the bathroom! I mean, this is right behind my seat. Before she shut the door, she looked around the corner, right at me, and smiled that gentle smile. Then, my seat began to shake as the bathroom vibrated. From what I could hear, and I could hear plenty, she enjoyed herself a lot better during the second round of "bo bo".

When she stepped out of the bathroom, her face was a little sweaty, and I couldn't help but notice that her boobs were practically popping out of her top. Unfortunately, the big Indian, I mean Native American, was right behind her and staring at me. "What you looking at white boy?"

As I already had discovered, things can go downhill real fast in Montana. Especially when she assured the scary dude that I was nothing compared to him. He started for me, and I had to act fast. The old women were yelling. I grabbed my fly rod case and swung it like a Louisville Slugger toward his face. I didn't do much damage because I missed and only hit his shoulder. Like I said, this dude was tall. The aluminum case bent like a blade of grass as I heard the graphite rod shatter, and the only thing I accomplished was making him drop the bottle.

Then, everything seemed to happen in slow motion. The green square bottle didn't break. It was plastic, and I stared at the label. Tahitian water with electrolytes and eight essential vitamins. As the eight essential vitamins slopped on the floor I wondered: what happened to the Jägermeister? The big guy was steamed up now and charged at me. But he slipped on the wet floor and went down. The pretty girl was quick, she sat on his chest and started to call him him 'baby.' Next thing I know, the bus driver grabbed the back of my shirt and was hauling me down the aisle. Thank goodness, he's protecting me, I thought. But, no, he threw me off the bus.

"Stay there. I've called the state troopers. Don't try to leave."

The state police! I didn't do anything!

"Yeah, right. You just assaulted a law enforcement official."

Law enforcement?

"Jim Lamouix is the head of security up at the Deer Lodge super max. You're lucky he didn't kill you. Just wait for the troopers." He gave me that slow eyeball roll again.

So, there I was, on the side of U.S. Route 90 with no money and without my fly rod or vest as the Running Dog pulled away. I choked on the black smoke cloud left by the Dog. I began walking through the hot wind and swirling litter. The next exit was probably miles away. I asked myself, how can this be happening? I just wanted to go fishing. But I didn't think for too long because a cruiser with flashing lights and siren pulled up real soon.

"Sir, halt, turn around slowly, and put your hands up where I can see them." This was loudly broadcast from the cruiser's speakers. I followed directions, got cuffed, and found myself in the backseat of the state police cruiser.

I tried to explain that this was just a big misunderstanding. But State Trooper William Pettibone cut me off and told me that he first had to inform me of my "Miranda" rights. Wait a minute! Pettibone? You bet, T.J. is his brother. What are the chances of that? Maybe I shouldn't have mentioned T.J. Of course, he called up his brother and here I am in the Missoula County holding cell. I'm thinking hard about the law school I'm supposed to start in two weeks. I'm not quite sure what I'm going to tell Yale or the law school's scholarship committee if this results in a conviction.

But, let me tell you. When I get out of here, I'm leaving Montana and I'm not coming back. I don't care how good the fly fishing is. It's no place for a white boy from the East. But I guess even Custer learned that. Eventually.

Chapter Five: *Evening Things*

There was nothing to like about the guy. It seemed a malignant thought in this paradise setting, so I brushed it aside and looked up at a mature bald eagle perched in the overhanging cottonwood. I pulled on the heavy oars and kept the driftboat cocked toward the bank. I pointed out the eagle. No interest.

"Jesus H. Christ, where are the fish?"

The sun slanted off the clear water as we drifted along an undercut bank littered with a few ancient cars. The old Fords and Packards represented a distant and failed attempt to protect the pasture from the river's steady erosion.

"Look at that for pollution, will you?" Pointing at the cars, he said, "The EPA would be all over you if you tried to protect your land now." His laughter rumbled.

Now I could hear the South Fork's force. The rolling river rock vibrated under the boat, in the deeper water. I knew a large brown hung underneath a drooping mountain ash and directed his cast.

As usual, he stood tall, ruggedly handsome, and burly in the bow, dominating the boat. He lifted his rod and sent the bright yellow fly line forward. "Now, just mend the line."

"Don't tell me to fucking mend. It'll ruin my float. There are no fish there. You're going too fast."

I suggested to his companion, a slight man sitting in the stern, to cast closer to the bush. In the slanting light we all saw the big fish rise up, open its white mouth, and swirl at the hopper.

"Aw, I set the hook too soon, didn't I?"

"We all do that when we see a big fish," I replied. "Don't worry. That was quite a sight. Good cast." I happily felt the simmering anger in the bow.

"Well, Dick, can we get some fish into the boat before we pull out for the night?"

He knew my name was Richard, but he enjoyed calling me "Dick." He thought it was funny. We didn't have a good history. He was the head of a lesser known computer company in California and his wife had been some cabinet member in D.C. As I explained to the younger guides, he had an alpha dog complex. Big, used to getting his way, and accustomed to success. Rarely a good combination on the river.

I guided only part time for the lodge, usually when the captains of industry pulled in with their underlings. I certainly wasn't hired for my strength or fly-fishing skill. The young college kids had it all over me in terms of casting an entire fly line, rowing a boat all day long, and knowing the river. But I was older, could keep up the conversation, and didn't take as much shit from the rich dudes. Some of these want-to-be Carnegies would chew up the BYU fresh-faced sophomore guides, and that could be ugly. I was supposed to add a little maturity and story-telling around the evening fire.

The lodge owner also thought my work experience was a draw. As I told some of the dudes, I was a Boston trial lawyer with a significant outdoor addiction. Trial lawyer was an exaggeration. I was an associate in the litigation department of a large Boston law firm. Most of my billable hours consisted of reviewing piles of boring discovery documents and taking lengthy depositions of corporate types. Only rarely did I get the adrenaline jolt of the courtroom. Still, as long as I billed two thousand hours a year during the bleak months, I could take most of the summer off while the partners played golf or sailed their yachts to Block Island. The thought of warm weather freedom was what carried me. When one law firm eventually tired of my long summer absences, I quit, took the summer off, and was hired by an equally prestigious firm in September. That firm rather liked telling would-be hires that one of its associates was able to spend summers as a fly-fishing guide. The firm trotted me out as a recruiting tool as it wooed gullible law school graduates from famous universities. This somewhat deceptive advertising was fine with me as long as I was free to escape each July 1st. The result was this part-time guiding gig in which I was usually paired up with the biggest bad-ass capitalist.

But it wasn't always like that. The year before was particularly memorable. The owner of the lodge was guiding Alpha Dog and his lawyer. I was assigned his twenty-two-year-old daughter. I was the envy of the guide crew because she was very easy on the eyes and, frankly, a better fisher than her father. The warm, overcast July day produced a slew of hatching PMDs and the fishing was easy. We hopped out front of the other boats and just hit the riffles. Given the heat we quickly pulled up to each gravel island, got out, and wet waded. When the hatch began to peter out, I slowly rowed against the current as she cast toward the banks. By mid-day, she took off her shirt and was down to her bikini top. By the time we were into the wilderness of the canyon, the top was off, and she smiled at me over her shoulder as I worked the oars. Some days guiding is a real pleasure.

She suggested taking a swim and I pulled into a small side channel with a couple of deep pools and hardly enough water to float the boat. As she perched on top of the bow, ready to take a dive into a long green pool, I suggested that she might not want to get her shorts wet. As I said, I was hired for my maturity. She laughed, wiggled out of her shorts, and displayed a breathtaking thong and rump. I couldn't wait to get back to the lodge, tell my fellow guides, and become the summer stud.

She immediately jumped into the water but not into the deep pool. Her ankle smacked the oval stones on the shallow lip of the pool and twisted badly. Her screams of pain shattered the Shangri-La of the small channel.

"It's broken! God, it hurts!"

The loud cries continued as I hefted her onto the bank, and inspected her slightly swollen ankle. Then I gently tried to get her damn shorts on.

"Oh, my God! It hurts so bad! Don't touch it! Is it broken?"

I could hear Alpha Dog's boat, complete with lodge owner, scrapping into the channel in response to her cries. Although she was not nearly as focused on the shorts as I, we managed to get her bottom covered before the rescue boat arrived. Unfortunately, the bikini top was still back in my drift boat, and Alpha Dog did not look upon me kindly when he arrived. I received no tip that day and not many calls from the lodge owner for the rest of the summer. Thereafter, Alpha always referred to me as "Dick." We didn't have a good history.

I knew that there was a good riffle just before the camp. I hadn't seen any boats for a while, so I knew any feeding trout had not been spooked. I put the boat along the far bank, floated by the outside of the riffle, then cranked the oars and swung up below the riffle and into the quieter water.

"Hell, Dick, that was some nice rowing. Didn't know you had it in you."

EVENING THINGS

I could see heads and tails in the riffle and more below the shelf. I quickly tied an odd, but effective, emerger-style fly called a Crippled Quigley onto both lines.

"Hey, Dick, they're eating PMDs. How about one of those?"

"The fish are not feeding on the duns. They are eating the flies right under the surface. This pattern will work well. Just watch it carefully. Who wants to fish the riffle and who wants to take the shelf?"

Without replying, Alpha waded to where the riffle ended and the water slid over a shelf into the deeper water. He knew that this was where the largest trout would wait for food. His cast was good, but he didn't see the first two fish rise to mouth his fly. I waded over quietly.

A big cutthroat slowly rose and sucked down the fly. I quietly said, "Take him."

Alpha raised his rod and was onto a good fish. He smiled, held his rod high, and yelled to his companion, "Fish on!"

The fish kept feeding and both sports landed a few. By the time we were back in the drift boat, everyone was smiling.

"Row us to camp Dick. It's time for a drink."

The sun was now off the water, and the evening began to cool. Alpha began to complain, once again, about the IRS. Last year he had bitterly denounced the federal tax system because he was being audited. The rumor was that he was now facing indictment on federal tax charges. As I let the current sweep us downriver, I wondered how crooked, or dumb, or both, one had to be to get caught cheating on their taxes by the IRS under the current Administration. It was well known that the IRS had become very passive in enforcing the tax laws under Reagan. It seemed ironic that this corporate big wig should be cursing the most conservative executive department in decades.

The overnight camp on the South Fork was in a pleasant cottonwood grove with white outfitter tents, a long outdoor table, and a large firepan. After unloading the clients, setting up the camp chairs, fixing them a scotch on the rocks with a splash, and laying out a plate of cheese and crackers, the real work began. Being the first to camp, my job was to unload my boat, stow it, and then start the charcoal. Soon everyone arrived, and the clients watched from their chairs, drinks in hand, while the guides stacked the Dutch ovens between the coals and cooked dinner.

"Hey, Dick," the familiar voice bellowed over the rest of the conversation, "You'd make someone a good wife. Too bad you can't guide as well as you cook."

I knew I had to break the uncomfortable silence that followed. So, I looked up from ladling the chicken cacciatore from the large cast iron pot and replied, "If that's a marriage proposal, I'll think it over. But I don't know if you could afford me." Relieved laughter followed, and conversation resumed covering the usual topics of the fishing, the river wildlife, and the incredible Western beauty.

After dinner, we stoked the fire. The guides finally had a chance to crack a beer and someone broke out a guitar. As the other guides fed the fire with driftwood collected during the day, I took the apple cobbler off the coals. I learned how to make this desert several years ago.

It was on the Middle Fork of the Salmon. I was pressed into service because a couple of guides suddenly came down with the flu. The Middle Fork draws its fair share of fishermen, but it has a very laid-back clientele with lots of vacationers who just want to run the rapids, soak in the hot springs, and watch the light play on the steep canyon walls. The regulars taught me Dutch oven cooking and gave me the best line on the rapids.

One wealthy Duluth retiree was on the trip with his two granddaughters. He told me that his wife had died nine months earlier and he thought the river and his two grandchildren would relieve his pain. I liked him immediately. He was an avid cribbage player and would play with his granddaughters during cocktail hour. The three would deal the cards, move the pegs, and drink carbonated grape juice. With each glass they toasted to the day, treating the juice like Dom Perignon. After dinner, I would join them, and we would play in teams of two.

On the third day, I persuaded them to float with me and try some fly fishing. After lots of laughing, flies were eventually cast near likely spots. Luckily the three caught one small westslope cutthroat apiece on large brightly colored dry flies. We stopped at a small stream, and the girls splashed and played. With that flat, but light, Midwest accent, he said "I truly, truly haven't had such a fun day in such a long, long time." He put his arm around my shoulders, pulled me toward him, and kissed me on the top of the head. That evening, he tried to put a roll of bills in my pocket. I refused and told him to keep his money and spend it on his two granddaughters. His old, but clear, blue eyes danced, "Oh, that I will do. But, as they say in Minnesota, I'll be evening things up with you."

At three the next morning, the older granddaughter, only fifteen years old, woke me and said that her grandfather was ill. I lit the lantern and entered his tent. Both girls sat at the end of their sleeping pads terrified. He could still talk but was badly slurring his words and obviously in pain.

The canyon was too steep where we camped for a helicopter to land. The only choice was to float him down to the Flying B Ranch with its small airstrip. We left in the half light, with him braced on a stretcher. Floating with reduced light through unfamiliar rapids was not pretty, and I apologized for the bumps and spins and occasional groundings. He gave a thumbs-up gesture when we first set off and gripped his younger granddaughter's hand. The fifteen-year old sat in the bow quietly staring back at her grandfather. Once through the first rapid, he said something I could not understand and tried to lift his thumb. After that, he was silent. I checked his ragged breathing a few times. As the light began to fill the sky, I finally pulled the raft up to the Flying B. The small plane would arrive in about a half hour.

The girls lifted the back of the stretcher, and I had the front. Once on land, they hugged each other and cried. Then the older girl walked over to me, stood tall, and looked me in the eye. "He's going to die, isn't he?"

"He might."

"He's going to, right?"

"Probably. But why don't you both hold his hands. He'll know you're there." And they did.

A few guests at the Flying B headed down to the river for some casts before breakfast. I stared at them and thought they looked silly.

He was not breathing by the time we loaded him and the girls into the small plane. Strangely, the bright red plane looked beautiful as it climbed above the canyon and turned in the morning sun toward Salmon.

EVENING THINGS

The Alpha and his buddies were getting liquored up and again grumbling about the federal bureaucracy.

"Hey, Dickie boy, aren't you one of those Massachusetts liberals? Do you paahk your caah in Haavaard Yahd?"

Eventually, all the clients wandered off to their tents and we doused the embers of the fire.

Around midnight I was woken by one of the younger guides.

"Hey, the asshole has a gun. You better deal with him."

Sure enough, he was stumbling around the camp with a large revolver in his right hand screaming a line from the movie *Patton*: "Rommel," he shouted, "I read your book!" He laughed with a deep rumble and repeated himself.

I told him to cut the crap and give me the gun. He looked over at me with a surprised expression and meekly handed me the large Colt.

It was a heavy weapon, and I asked where the safety was. He quickly grabbed the gun from me, stepped back two paces, and slowly raised the revolver, first lingering the barrel on me and then pointing it up into the air. He pulled the trigger, a flame roared from the barrel, and the shot woke up the rest of the camp. He laughed again, looking at the small red embers falling against the star-filled sky.

I swung a heavy driftwood branch onto his forearm and he dropped the gun. I scooped it up, tossed it into the bushes, and, still armed with the driftwood, suggested that he return to his tent. His slender fishing companion led him away.

He spun around one last time, and bellowed, as if announcing some ageless truth or clever rejoinder, "Rommel, I read your book you brilliant bastard!"

As expected, he was quiet and hung-over during breakfast. We cooked up huevos rancheros and Dutch oven coffee cake. Despite the strong cowboy coffee and the brilliant day, it seemed as if a cool fog hung over all the guests.

But, even prodigious amounts of Dewars couldn't keep him down for long. A young female doctor asked the Alpha to pass the pepper.

Again, the big voice, "You bet your sweet patootie, I'll pass this pepper. And, young lady, you do have one sweet patootie, you spicy little thing."

She rolled her eyes, looked over to me as if I was this man's keeper, stood up and left the table.

"Hell," he rumbled, "What did I do? I was just giving her a compliment."

I quietly approached the doctor a few minutes later, apologized, and promised that tomorrow I would guide her on a solitary trip up a fine stream. He hustled up behind me and, somewhat to my surprise, quietly, said: "Look Doc, I didn't mean any offense. I'm just an old dog and I don't learn new tricks quickly. I made you feel uncomfortable and I regret it. My ex-wife, bless her heart, would be kicking me in the teeth for that comment. No wonder she's my ex. Please accept my full apology." He must have succeeded in business for a reason because the doctor laughed, and they shook hands.

As I was loading the drift boat, he climbed into the rear seat and said:

"Look buddy, I am very sorry about last night. Too much to drink. I don't know what got into me."

EVENING THINGS

He stayed in the less desirable stern seat all day, sometimes casting, sometimes just leaning back and watching the hawks wheel in the sky. He couldn't bring himself to call me by name but didn't call me "Dick" all day. He tipped me generously.

Two weeks later he was dead. An overdose of sleeping pills mixed with large amounts of alcohol. I pulled into the large riffle and tied on a Cripple Quigley, thinking of his rumbling laugh and the young doctor shaking his hand.

In late September, Federal Express delivered an overnight package to the lodge. A West Coast law firm explained the wishes of the deceased and enclosed a small portion of his ashes in a heat-sealed plastic packet. They were to be spread on the South Fork. The lodge owner tried not to smile as he handed me the packet. "It's the perfect job for you. Sorry the daughter isn't here to help."

It was my last trip of the season. I had to get back to my real job. The sun was bright and the wind had a cold bite. The fishing was slow, but the client caught a few. In the late afternoon, I couldn't put off the task any longer. I set the client up in the middle of a not particularly good riffle and walked to the tail out with the small packet. I tried to think kind thoughts about the man, but nothing much came to mind. It all seemed dismal. No family or corporate underlings present, no nice words of remembrance. Hell, I thought, his ashes would probably wash down into some diversion ditch and end up on a potato field. At least he would have been happy that I was dropping a pollutant into a navigable water in violation of the Clean Water Act. I emptied the packet into the current. One small clump floated near the bank. The sparkling chop made it difficult to see, but I swear a trout rose to it.

Chapter Six: *Distant Lands*

Being white as chalk, it was not easy to walk into a crowded bar in Roxbury. I looked around the smoky room as faces turned from watching the Celtics and slowly filled with suspicion. As I took three steps into the bar, looking left and right, a tall lanky man pushed back his chair from a table and blocked my way. He rose to his height of about six foot six and asked, "Are you a cop?" The hostility in his voice did not surprise me. After all, this was Boston in the late 1970s and racial tension seared the city. This reception produced a noticeable heartbeat and some perspiration. Dressed in jeans and a sweater, I still carried a briefcase because I expected my client to hand over various documents relating to the case. I held up the briefcase like a passport or as definitive evidence of being a complete nerd; no police officer would be caught dead with such an item. I spluttered, "No, I'm a lawyer. I'm here to meet Ben Washington."

Apparently, the briefcase did the trick. "Hey," the lanky man turned and yelled, "Ben, here's your lawyer. Hey, everybody, Ben has his very own white lawyer!"

Ben's laughter was louder and deeper than any of the other audience members. He motioned for me to join him at the bar. Ben was a big man with a big smile. He clapped me on the back and introduced me to T.J. and Sam, some of the other class members. With the tolerance and hesitant support of my downtown law firm, I was representing Ben in a class action lawsuit alleging that a major Boston manufacturer, the largest employer in the city, had systematically practiced employment discrimination based on race. Ben was the so-called "class representative" whose most patriotic name, Benjamin Roosevelt Washington, appeared on the court papers. The lawsuit claimed that the company had discriminated against Ben and hundreds of other "similarly situated" African Americans, like T.J. and Sam.

Ben handed over the documents and various witness statements and walked me to my car, a beat-up Volkswagen Rabbit. When we reached my vehicle, Ben chuckled and put a hand on my shoulder and squeezed, "Well brother, no one is going to steal this piece of shit. Why you driving this crap when you work where you do?"

Ben and I had become friendly, and he visited my office occasionally. Ben, dressed in his casual work clothes, would receive some stares from the corporate types, entrepreneurs, and trust clients who shared the sleek waiting area. More stares followed when Ben greeted me with his usual "power to the people" handshake and an enveloping hug.

The partners, to their credit, were tolerant of my client and the lawsuit. This from an old-line law firm that had rejected Louis Brandeis' employment application and featured partners with *first* names like Aldrich, Weld, Brooks, and Rhodes. In fact, these same partners had subsidized the hefty fees of my expert statistician and the escalating expenses of numerous depositions. Perhaps the firm wanted to showcase its commitment to pro bono work, or further my appeal as a recruiting tool, or was bowing to the wishes of the managing partner who, luckily enough, had taken me under his wing. The firm's largesse, however, was my burden. I trudged along on this solitary road with fear, worry, and pride constantly cycling through my brain. I did the research, the drafting, the arguing, and the footwork. And I found myself spending a considerable amount of time in the mostly black neighborhoods of Roxbury and Mattapan.

On his visits, Ben usually sank into a chrome and leather chair and looked around my office and out to the impressive view of

Boston Harbor. When I first met with him and explained the case, I asked if he had any questions. He did, "Let's get this straight," he swiveled his head, looking around my office, and then gestured down the hallway that contained a row of larger offices for the partners, "you are 'the Man', but you're going to represent me and stick it to 'the Man'?"

I lifted an eyebrow and replied, "I guess that's one way to put it."

Ben smiled, "Well I like that. But why are you doing this for me and the others?"

"Honestly, I went to law school to do things like this. As corny as it sounds, I became a lawyer to help people."

Ben laughed, "If I was a lawyer, I'd concentrate on making money!"

"Oh, they pay me well enough," I replied and thought of the phone conversation I had with my father soon after starting with this firm. To my surprise he asked me what my salary was. When I told him that, with the expected year-end bonus, I might make north of thirty thousand my father, the author of several books and chairman of a college history department, gasped and admitted, "After all these years, I've never made that high a salary." He paused, apparently trying to regain parental ground, and then gave way to the relief of knowing that he would never again have to financially support his son. He had received the godsend that every parent yearns for: the child was fledged and on his way. My father cheerfully added, "You already know that money isn't everything, but, Rich, it sure is something."

When the case was close to trial, Ben and I met several times to prepare his testimony. After one long session, Ben looked at a photo on my desk and asked, "Is that you doing some kind of fishing?"

"Yeah, Ben, I was fly fishing for trout."

"Never done that. Do you do that often?"

I looked at the picture, "Not in over a year. I've been working too hard." Then an idea struck me, "When this case is over, why don't we go up to the Merrimack River and fish for some striped bass?"

Ben's laugh rolled out, "You want *this* black man to do *that* kind of fishing up north? Let's get real. You come on over to my house for Sunday dinner this weekend. I'm smoking ribs. Time for *you* to be in the minority."

The first floor of a tired three decker was filled with Ben's friends plus assorted children, his three and various others. Ben manned the smoker in the backyard, handed me a Bud, and introduced me to a group of his neighbors. This group was friendly, but reserved. Ben gave no explanation as to why this white guy had suddenly appeared. Given the segregated nature of Boston's neighborhoods, whites rarely walked the Roxbury streets unless they were cops or school children subject to court-ordered bussing. The men who clustered around Ben nodded to me or muttered a greeting, but basically treated me as if I carried a contagious disease.

Feeling like a smiling alien who had parachuted from outer space, I left the backyard and wandered into the kitchen. There I met Ben's wife, Ariel. She was almost the opposite of Ben. Thin, with a much lighter complexion than Ben's nearly black skin, and a downturned mouth and tired expression.

"You must be Ben's lawyer."

"Good guess." I extended my hand and she shook it limply, avoided my gaze, and then went back to chopping cabbage. "Let me help you," I offered.

She looked up with mild surprise, "That's the first offer to help I've received all day. Can you finish chopping this cabbage while I make up a slaw dressing?"

As I chopped, I asked how she had met Ben. She had grown up in this neighborhood and had known him most of her life. They had an on and off relationship in high school, "The typical story, he was a football player, and I was a cheerleader."

I looked at her, dressed in sweat pants and a baggy T-shirt, and could not imagine that this slight woman with a drawn face was once a smiling, bouncy cheerleader.

She continued, "You must know by now that Ben could charm the leaves off the trees. He was quite the ladies' man and his friends follow him like the Pied Piper." She sighed, "Hell, he convinced me to drop out of Oberlin after two years and I've been in this kitchen ever since." She looked at the ceiling and made an angry sound, "What a fool I am."

She changed gears suddenly, "You know Ben got screwed by that company. He was doing a great job working the line, then he applied for a supervisor position and they rejected him and made his life hell. Thank God he got a good job at Wang supervising production, but it was a tough two years before that."

I nodded, "That's what the lawsuit is all about. The company did that over and over again. It would hire African Americans for the low-level manufacturing jobs and never promote them to line supervisor or any higher position."

She snorted, "African American? Is that what you folks call us? Hell, Ben and I didn't come from Africa. My family has been here in the United States since the country started. You can just call me 'black'. I'm American, not African." She paused and seemed to be enjoying this burst of anger, "How ridiculous. I thought you were educated. What are you European American?"

"Point taken," I reminded myself to be patient and replied, "I used the term African American because right now it's considered the most politically correct."

Ariel gave a look of disgust and turned her head, "It's just an example of your white guilt."

My reminder to be patient vanished. I was working an exhausting number of hours. I had a day job defending corporate America followed by a late-night shift representing Ben and the class. It all made me cranky, and I quickly responded without the slightest diplomacy, "I'm not working on this case because I feel any guilt. I just think that discrimination is wrong, and, luckily, it's illegal. I wouldn't care if the discrimination was because you're black, purple, or ugly. It's unfair and it pisses me off and, having gone to law school, I know the levers to pull in order to fight it. That's why I'm busting my butt. But guilt? You've got the wrong guy."

The words flowed from me without any effort or thought, as if I had opened a faucet. After my tirade, I felt spent and a bit surprised. For the first time, Ariel smiled, "Now I can understand why Ben likes you so much. How about finishing that chopping so we can eat?"

The ribs were delicious. We ate around a couple of folding tables in the backyard. Kids running around and the adults bent over paper plates and eating the ribs with their hands, reaching for the roll of paper towels, and asking for more of Ariel's spicy sauce. It reminded me of my youth in southern Virginia when we would visit or host Mrs. Dexter and her large family for Sunday dinner. The fact that my mother called the black woman who, twice weekly, helped her care for the increasing brood of children "Mrs.", humored our white neighbors in the still officially segregated south of the early 1950s. They probably laughed it off as some peculiar custom of the North until they noticed the unthinkable hosting of a large black family for dinner. Even though this was a small enclave of college professors, the attitude toward my parents cooled considerably. The fact that my father subscribed to the liberal *New Republic* magazine and taught the Civil War and Reconstruction periods with a revisionist slant did not help matters. After a few years, and to my parents' relief, we left the Virginia Military Institute and the Old Dominion and headed north. As we settled into a colder climate, I distinctly remember missing three things: seeing my father in his military dress uniform as he went off to teach, roughhousing with Mrs. Dexter's children, and staring at the stuffed version of Stonewall Jackson's horse 'Little Sorrel'.

I was quite sure that sharing any of these memories of white privilege, liberal leanings, and Confederate memorabilia with Ben and his friends would not help my standing. I had not thought of Mrs. Dexter in years and had never considered how the woman balanced raising her own children while still helping my mother for what must have been a minimal paycheck. I was quite sure Ben or Ariel had never had the benefit of a Mrs. Dexter. And I could not imagine a young Ben staring at the moth eaten, taxidermized horse ridden by a fanatical, blue-eyed traitor. Maybe, I thought, I should be registering some white guilt. I, however, was too tired to feel much of anything. As the party broke up, I climbed into my battered Rabbit and wearily headed back to my high-rise office to further prepare for the upcoming trial.

The case settled on the eve of trial. This was no shock given the strength of the case and the damaging publicity that the company would have incurred during a long, well publicized federal recounting of racial animus and stereotypes. The offer to settle, and the generous terms, disappointed me because I was fully prepared to present compelling evidence of this Fortune 500 company's extensive history of discrimination. More to the point, I was looking forward to the courtroom spotlight. Not caring if the settlement floundered, I drove a hard bargain and obtained a result that exceeded any possible courtroom judgment. As the class representative, Ben received all the salary he lost by not getting the promotion plus a generous bonus for his efforts in bringing the suit. The class members, such as T.J. and Sam, were awarded a pool of one million dollars to be divided according to the financial loss each suffered by not receiving the desired promotions. In addition, much to the relief of the law firm partners, the company was to pay my hefty legal fees and expenses.

It is rare for an associate to win a substantial case, garner good publicity, and fill the firm's coffers with a fee and expense award exceeding two hundred thousand dollars. Various partners congratulated me or looked at me with some interest knowing that I had helped their bottom line.

My first call was to Ben. I explained the pending settlement and obtained his approval. He told me to meet him at his favorite Roxbury bar that evening to celebrate, and I promised to buy a round for the house. "You're my man," he responded. When I entered the bar, Ben strode up, gave me a hard hug, and then leaned back while still holding me, "Thank you. I never thought anyone would care, but…" His voice broke and he hugged me harder. I hugged him back, told him that he was a great guy and that I was happy to help.

"Hey Ben," shouted a voice, "stop the homo stuff." Ben and I both laughed and let go of each other. I felt as though the sun was shining and that all the work of law school and the grind of this case was a small price for this moment.

I slapped hands with Sam and other class members. T.J., who still worked at the company and stood to gain over sixty thousand, held up his glass of Remy Martin and happily said, "It's like Christmas twice over."

A week later, Ben and Ariel met me at my office to pick up his settlement check of $76,000. After handing over the check to Ben, I told them that I had just decided to leave the firm and join the U.S. Attorney's Office as a criminal prosecutor. Ben looked stunned, glanced around the plush office and out the window to Boston Harbor, "Are they forcing you out because of this case?"

I assured Ben that the job move was entirely my choice. He shook his head, "You're kidding, right? Why would you ever give up this sweet spot?"

I explained that my dream since graduating from law school was to be an Assistant U.S. Attorney. Ben shook his head, "You're going to take a government job over this? Do they pay better than this gig?"

I smiled, "Actually I'm taking a big pay cut."

"Man", Ben responded, "you are just one crazy white dude."

I made a reservation at a fancy French restaurant for a celebratory lunch. As we sat in the courtyard ordering a bottle of Bordeaux from the wine sommelier, I leaned back and silently thanked my luck and the firm's expense account. As was usual, Ben dominated the conversation during lunch, and Ariel sat quietly. Waiting for coffee and desert, Ben stood, stretched and announced that he was heading to the men's room.

As he headed off whistling, Ariel flatly said, "He's just going to smoke a joint. This gives me a chance to tell you something."

I smiled, thought of Ben in a cloud of marijuana smoke as a Brahmin banker walked into the men's room. Then I drank my last sip of wine and asked, "What's up?"

Ariel shifted in her chair and looked directly at me, "You used Ben. You settle the case, hand out some checks, and get all this praise like you're the great, white father. Still, I see through you. You got much more money from this case than Ben. You can sit pretty in your fancy office and take any job you want, even if it pays less. But our lives won't change. Ben and I will still be working like dogs trying to pay the bills."

It took a little time to respond because her hard tone was a complete surprise, "I negotiated a big award for Ben. He got all the money he would have received from the promotion he bid on until he got the much higher paying job at Wang. Then I made sure he got a 50 thou bonus. That's damn good."

She was prepared with a quick retort, "Not as good as what you got out of it."

"Ariel," I explained, "the fee award goes to the firm. I don't get that money. And some of that award just repays the firm for expenses it paid while I prepared for trial." Ariel sat stone faced, and I added, "Look $76,000 is about twice what I make in a year."

Ariel continued to stare at me, "Seventy-six thou is chump change. You used Ben. I hope you know that."

I tried to explain, "Ariel, it's not like winning the lottery. A lawsuit is about recovering your damages."

"Chump change," she repeated.

It was as if we came from far distant lands with different languages. We were not communicating and not understanding the other. Perhaps each of us was speaking the truth in part, but neither could begin to grasp that possibility. Obviously, I had not taken the advice of the patron saint of lawyers, Atticus Finch. I had not walked around for a while in Ariel's shoes, but then maybe Ariel's shoes, filled with anger and regret, would never fit. As I looked somewhat dumbfounded at Ariel, I could see that she had built a wall I could never climb over.

"Huh," Ben returned and his smile was fading, "I see that Ariel spoke her mind."

I looked up at him and said, "Ben, we should all talk about this."

"Ben," Ariel raised her voice, "it's time to go. Now."

Ben looked at me, opened his eyes wide, shrugged his big shoulders, "We're good brother, but I got to go."

Ben and Ariel left without looking back at me. I felt hurt, confused, and angry, like some bad romantic breakup. I felt tears well in my eyes. I swiped at them and asked for the check.

I called Ben and Ariel three times and left messages. The messages were not returned.

Later that month, I walked home to my apartment in Boston's once charming South End. This somewhat frayed and tired neighborhood was on the cusp of being claimed by affluent yuppies. It was late. I had been wrapping up work at the firm. Because of the darkness, I did not cut across the Boston Common, but stayed on the well-lighted streets sprinkled with the sad, muttering homeless. I knew that the night often scratched off the thin veneer of civilization. Just last week, I had scared off a midnight cat burglar who slipped into a fourth-floor window while I lay in bed. When the police arrived, I described the large man who was armed with a carving knife taken from my kitchen. The two officers looked at each other and confirmed that it was probably the same man who had lowered himself from a roof and entered an apartment two doors down. He anally raped the male occupant. Hell, I thought, I might not be cut out for this gentrification business; I'd rather take my chances with a mother grizzly.

I was seriously thinking about fleeing the city. I missed living where chickadees chattered, and red tails flew. And, I needed a break. I thought of wading a clear freestone stream where the rocks looked like gems under the water.

Two young black men wearing gray hoodies interrupted my thoughts. They ambled in front of me and blocked my way. Then they began to hassle me. One began to move toward my back.

Maybe it was my lingering disappointment over the unreturned calls, maybe it was temporary lunacy, but I raised my voice, "Hey, don't fuck with me, I'm the Man!" Then I lifted my briefcase like a torch, "And I'm an attorney!"

The two men hesitated and backed off slightly. I brushed by them and quickened my pace. I heard one say to the other, "That's one crazy white dude."

As I jogged away, I smiled and thought of Ben.

Chapter Seven: *Looking for Mr. Right*

The pursuit of happiness in this materialistic age often includes owning a vacation home in some near-paradise setting. The Internal Revenue Code, with its seductive mortgage deductions, encourages the few remaining in the comfortable middle class to enjoy the extravagance of a shingled cottage overlooking the Atlantic, an old camp in the Adirondacks, a condo on Sanibel Island, a pre-fab log cabin on the Rouge River, or a slope-side time-share in Breckenridge.

It is a dream of leisure and relaxation: recharging the proverbial batteries while lounging on a deck in a magnificent setting while most of your countrymen work dead-end jobs and lead lives closer to Willie Lowman's than John D. Rockefeller's. It is a dream of escaping a world that no longer seems as promising, safe, or understandable as when "Leave It to Beaver" first aired. And to many, the dream encompasses a desire to be accepted into the community and culture of that chosen paradise. In the fuzzy language of sociology, these comfortable interlopers are striving for social acceptance. Or more simply put: Who wants to be viewed as some honky tourist, some dude, some off-islander?

After fifteen years of practicing law, I decided to live such a dream and take a sabbatical. I had been groomed at a venerable, fancy-pants Boston law firm with pretty paralegals and cushy offices, before fleeing to become a hard-bitten federal prosecutor. For a decade, I punctured egos and imprisoned the well-heeled frauds who bilked the gullible, pillaged the government purse, or screwed the environment.

It wasn't all long hours and hard work. Maybe I had watched too many Frank Capra movies, but I found it exciting and moving to stand before a jury and begin the opening of a criminal trial with the words: "My name is Richard Wales, and I represent the United States of America." Talk about waving the flag. Also, in Boston, there is something immensely satisfying about having some legal Brahmin with the last name of Lowell or Adams or Hancock seek to avoid indictment by telling you, "My ancestors and your ancestors came to this Commonwealth centuries ago and they would be shocked to see how uncaring you and the federal government have become." Then, with an incongruous combination of beseechment and arrogance, this partner of an old-line law firm could not resist making some remark about the irresponsible, young, impertinent "mongrels" that now populate the U.S. Attorney's Office. These types of encounters put enough wind in your sails and irritation in your gut to power you along for several years. But the thrill had worn off. I was catching a whiff of Willie Lowman-like ennui.

After all, I liked the word "sabbatical." It provided such a prestigious and serious tone to goofing off. In my case, "sabbatical" was just a fancy word for doing nothing for three months while collecting no pay. The federal government even has an acronym for this type of laziness: LWOP, leave without pay. I immediately used this abbreviation to christen my drift boat.

My behavior was hardly an example of Max Weber's Protestant work ethic, and the prospect considerably troubled my New England father who had lived through the Depression and watched his father declare bankruptcy. He envisioned his only son throwing away years of education and training in the pursuit of becoming a bum. "What are you going to do for three months—just fish, eat and drink?" I had too much love and respect for him to provide the simple three-letter answer.

But first, I needed an exotic locale in which to vegetate. There were ample choices: the Dalles in Oregon, a cabin in Maine, maybe

LOOKING FOR MR. RIGHT

Telluride or Bozeman, or perhaps Menemsha on Martha's Vineyard. I chose Tetonia, Idaho.

Tetonia? That's right. It is a Mormon church, a post office, gas station/convenience store, and a café, together with 198 people, a couple of grain silos, an abandoned Union Pacific line, and many acres of potatoes and barley. You will not find it listed in any travel brochures.

My choice of towns was primarily based on my wallet and Tetonia's location in Pierre's Hole. Pierre's Hole, named after a culturally mixed, energetic Canadian trapper from the 1820s, is now known, in this less poetic and more commercial age, as "Teton Valley"—apparently so named by Chamber of Commerce sorts who thought that people could be lured to the Tetons but not to a hole.

Like many beautiful portions of the Rocky Mountain west, Pierre's Hole sits on the cusp of a recreational boom. The larger towns in the valley, Driggs and Victor, stand to profit commercially, if not aesthetically, from the threatened expansion of the nearby ski area. Tempers flare between pro- and anti-development factions. But the debate is academic in Tetonia. Tucked in the valley's northern corner, Tetonia is not a boom-or-bust town. It is all bust. That is what attracted me. That and also the fact that the name reminded me of something out of a Marx Brothers film.

The realtor lifted her eyebrows when I pointed to the tiny cabin and announced that it was perfect. She earlier had referred to it, in a rather demeaning tone, as the "Hobbit House." With its octagonal design, steep pitched roof, and hut-like quality, it did seem to step from the pages of J.R.R. Tolkien. What if it was only one room and a small loft? Low maintenance. Or, so I thought.

After purchasing the place over a long winter weekend and jetting back to the East Coast, it occurred to me that the long distance owning of a dream cabin created some logistical problems. Who was to sweep out the dirt, buy a refrigerator, or turn on the water? My idea of a sabbatical did not include these tasks. Again, my realtor came to the rescue and sent me a business card she noticed posted on the bulletin board in the local market. "Randy Right—Odd Jobs of All Types." The card contained a design of two capital Rs facing each other. At the bottom of the card was the slogan, "The right man for the job." I called immediately.

Sure enough, Randy Right did it all and more. Within the month, the windows were sparkling, the floor was clean, a second-hand refrigerator and stove were installed, the water was flowing, and the second-hand furniture was in place. He also called to tell me the bad news. He wanted to know why I had bought a place without a driveway. I neglected to consider the absence of any means of egress during the rapid purchase given the three feet of snow on the ground. He also inquired whether he should replace all the missing and ripped shingles on the roof. Again, that damn snow. And what should he do about the large gaps between the logs that were now being used by chipmunks as entrance doors. How had I missed this obvious defect?

I immediately inquired about local workmen who could put in a gravel road, install a new roof, and chink the walls. Most everyone was pretty busy, I was told. But, no need to worry, Mr. Right could do it all. Being no fool, I asked for an estimate. "Well tough to tell. A lot depends on the supplies and the time it takes, but I'll do right by you." After all, I reasoned, what good is paradise without a little trust? I promptly sent off a fat check to cover materials.

I arrived and my high spirits were not dampened by the fact that the road was only half complete. Anyway, it was a rental and the car could take a few bumps. The roof also looked suspiciously unfinished and whatever chinking had been done did not prevent chipmunks from scampering into the dwelling during the day or a horde of moths from entering each night.

Mr. Right visited on the evening of my arrival and offered a warm, firm handshake. Then, somewhat shyly, he presented me with two pillows that his wife had made. "We wanted to welcome you proper to the valley, and we knew you liked fishing." The pillows, sporting a fringe of polyester lace, depicted massive, open-jawed, largemouth bass—a species foreign to the Rocky Mountains—chomping on terrified, fleeing minnows. I honestly stated that I had never seen pillows like these and, then, perhaps less honestly, pronounced them beautiful and promised to display them prominently. Unlike many promises, I had to keep this one. Since there was so much unfinished construction work, I knew Randy would be present to notice the pillows at frequent intervals.

As Randy Right was leaving, I inquired about the driveway and roof. He was sure glad that I had brought that up. You see, he was real sorry, but it was a much bigger job than expected. Also, he had to visit his elderly parents in Salt Lake this weekend, and he sure could use an extra advance for gas and a small present for the folks. I nodded, thought of the pillows and the elderly parents, and trundled off toward my checkbook.

Randy promised to be back real soon to finish up the work, and he added that he had to take me to a secret spot where trout came on every cast. I waved goodbye as the sun set behind the Tetons. The aspens rustled in a soft breeze. It seemed so perfect.

Needless to say, I didn't see a trace of Mr. Right for weeks.

In the meantime, I lived out my father's fears and simply rambled and fished every day. The Henry's Fork, the South Fork of the Snake, and the Teton: fabulous and famous water, but not easy to fish and sometimes downright difficult. I was sorely in need of a bit of local advice. There was only one sporting goods store in the valley, presided over by the ever-genial Nick Christian. I knew Nick as a hard-working, knowledgeable, friendly fishing guide. Certainly he would take pity on an outsider who was desperately in need of insider information.

It was difficult, however, to get Nick to talk fishing. Since my visit the previous summer, he had become enamored with a miracle product known as Melaleuca. An hour's explanation followed. This miracle potion was refined from a plant native to southern Australia and used to tremendous effect in products ranging from toothpaste, skin cream, and shampoo to tile cleaner, laundry detergent, shampoo, and insect repellant. I left lugging a two-gallon jug of bathroom cleaner (dilute with five parts water to one part Melaleuca—enough to last through the twenty-first century at the small Hobbit House), two tubes of tooth polish (with an acidic taste that truly opened your eyes in the morning), mosquito repellant, and a few flies.

Having failed to obtain any local secrets, I waded the beautiful rivers, gazed at the sky, watched sandhill cranes and eagles fly, confronted moose, deer, and gray owls, and caught more than my fair share of fish.

As the summer progressed, one of my many sisters arrived for a visit. She looked about the Hobbit House, with its scurrying chipmunks and fluttering moths, and pronounced it a dump. When she asked why I had bought a cabin in such a desolate location, I assured her that I had purchased it for the same price as a two-week Caribbean cruise. Her response was the expected, "you should have gone to the Caribbean."

LOOKING FOR MR. RIGHT

Being a contrarian, I loved the valley and grew to appreciate the quirky nature of the cabin. The local gas attendant, café waitress, banker, and liquor store clerk came to know me by name. The smiling, heavy set liquor store clerk was convinced that I, despite vigorous denials, was a modest poet hard at work. The gas attendant arrived at a somewhat different conclusion of my profession after an FBI agent, wishing to deliver some allegedly urgent report by hand, came to town and asked for my address. As the young man filled my tank, he confided in a quiet tone, "Don't worry Richard, I didn't tell him anything about you. Said I never heard of you. What you do is nobody's business. We all got to make a living, you know." He punched me on the shoulder after handed him cash for the gas.

By September, the waitress at the local café always smiled and knew my breakfast order without asking: a "Woody," a concoction of eggs, sausage, cheese, and potatoes. As I sat in the café enjoying this cholesterol laden dish, I listened to all the chatter that surrounded me. Apparently, there had been a big dance the night before to benefit a child in the valley diagnosed with leukemia. Everyone at the café, except me, had been there. As I looked around at the weather worn faces of the ranchers and the younger expatriates from the East who had now set down roots in this valley, I felt like the outsider I was. These folks could not have been friendlier, but I was not one of them.

With this bittersweet thought, I headed off to roam the golden aspens of the foothills. Late that afternoon, I put on my best prosecutorial demeanor and knocked on Randy Right's door to inquire when the hell he would finish the work I had paid for. Enough of being some friendly cash machine. Randy's five-year-old daughter answered the door and immediately hugged my leg.

"Mommy, Uncle Richie's here." Uncle Richie? Maybe this longing for social acceptance was not all that it was cracked up to be.

But there was no time to reflect. Dinner was on the table. Randy's ever understanding wife pulled me in to partake in one of those meals that you thought had disappeared with Norman Rockwell: fresh baked biscuits, homemade jam, stuffed chicken, peach pie, blessings, and many children underfoot. I left with belly bulging as the entire Right household waved me off. During the entire evening, the conversation never remotely drifted toward any financial topic.

The day before I left for Boston, one of Randy's towheaded children appeared at the cabin door carrying a jar of the raspberry jam that I had complimented during dinner.

Upon my return to Logan Airport, I confronted snarled traffic, dismal tank farms, and enraged drivers. During my three-month escape, I had not missed this urban anger fest. Even though Boston is often a charming city, blessed with a stunning harbor and beautiful architecture, many of its long-time inhabitants bear a grudge against the world. It is as though they are still pissed off at Ted Williams's refusal to leave the dugout and tip his hat after ending his Fenway career by hitting a home run.

The next week I summoned in a young lawyer engaged in a corrupt conspiracy. When he and his counsel arrived at the Office of the United States Attorney, I confronted him with the evidence, and presented him with the stark choice of being disbarred from his profession and cooperating at trial or spending the rest of his twenties in a federal penitentiary. His lawyer explained that his client was a low-level associate, a recent graduate of a small-time law school who was in awe of the Harvard-educated partners. I countered with the young lawyer's repeated fraudulent statements and his eager entry into the scheme. Eyes watering, the young man interrupted his lawyer and stammered, "Everyone was doing it. Can't you give me another choice?" His lawyer tried to calm him into silence by touching his arm and shaking his head.

His lawyer's gestures didn't work. When I demanded a plea to a federal felony charge, the young law firm associate erupted, "You, sir, are a hard man." I apparently had spent too long out West for my reply sounded like Louis L'Amour dialogue, "Sir, it's a hard life."

His counsel took over, and, after quick negotiations, I knew that this young lawyer's testimony would bring down an old-line Boston law firm that had been engaging in bank fraud for a decade. It would shake the Boston legal establishment and enrage local bar associations. This would be fun. I was back in the saddle again.

On the train ride home, I thought of the young attorney and the hard choices of life. As I stared out the window, my mind grimly wandered to the cabin's still leaking roof, the driveway that resembled a goat path, and other ongoing expenses of the Hobbit House. I vowed to call Randy that night. Then I let out a long breath and thought of sandhill cranes lit by the setting sun as they flew across the valley. I studied my reflection in the train window and noticed a small smile. As my visiting sister reminded me, the maintenance problems of a second home are plainly "a first world problem." I wasn't that young lawyer facing professional ruin and a felony charge, or a crack-addicted child with no real home, or the survivor of some African famine or genocide. I fully realized that my exasperation with Mr. Right was hardly the stuff of a Blind Lemon Jefferson blues song.

I closed my eyes and envisioned the little Hobbit House surrounded by golden aspens. It really wasn't that I wanted to be accepted as some Western local. Rather, I wanted to find a place where I could recapture the excitement and innocence of my blessed childhood. It probably was an impossible quest, but I was damn lucky to be able to try. I knew that I wouldn't make the confrontational telephone call. I could still taste the summer in that jar of raspberry jam.

Chapter Eight: *Way Up on Slough*

It is rare that you learn the worth of your life to the precise penny. It can be a disappointment.

The call came on a beautiful Saturday afternoon in late September. One of those days with cloudless blue skies, dry air, the promise of football games, and scarlet leaves.

Kent Powers, a veteran of the FBI, repeated: "The contract is for $25,000. He's already paid half and will pay the other half when you're dead."

I looked out the window and watched a chipmunk wrestling with an acorn.

I didn't know how to respond, but finally I blurted, "That's all I'm worth, 25 thou?"

"Hey, that's above the going rate. Most contracts are for 20 thousand. I guess you cost more because you're a fed."

Kent and I had been investigating a massive bank fraud case where a group of organized crime guys had gotten to the bank president and were draining the bank of funds while, at the same time, laundering lots of cash through the bank. The bank's vice president also was involved, but we had turned him, placed him and his family into the witness protection program, and started up a wiretap. It was a big case for the FBI and the U.S. Attorney's Office.

"I thought only the Columbians went after prosecutors. How did you hear about this?"

Kent, like so many agents, had a flat Midwestern voice that sounded like a watered down version of Tom Brokaw. "I guess you're just lucky. The State Police have an informant who tipped us off. Then, we confirmed it by chatter on the wiretap. We have to move on this. Can you pack a bag and meet us at your office in an hour?"

"Pack a bag? Where am I going?"

"Well, you can't stay at your home. They already gave your address to the shooter."

Gave my address to the shooter. That is the type of statement that focuses one's attention real quick. "I'll be there in an hour."

My office was crowded when I arrived. The U.S. Attorney was there, and the boss's presence on a late Saturday afternoon meant that this was serious business. He grasped my hand and said, "Hey, we're not in Kansas anymore, Toto." I weakly smiled. The FBI Assistant Special Agent in Charge, a guy I had never trusted, slid forward, punched me on the upper arm, and said, "Sorry this had to happen to a good guy like you. We'll get these bastards." Kent rolled his eyes in the background.

Seeing Kent cheered me. "So, speaking of the bastards, why don't we just pick up whoever put out the contract, and, for good measure, arrest this would-be assassin?" I asked. The ASAC slid away and looked over to Kent.

Unfortunately, the bank president and the crime boss were, to use Kent's phrase, "in the wind." The phone taps had gone quiet and the primary targets had disappeared.

I absorbed this piece of news, but surprised myself by thinking clearly and asking the next obvious question, "Well, can't we pick up the hired gun? We have enough to hold him based on the informant."

Again, heads turned to Kent. Grimacing, he said, "The State doesn't want to burn its informant; this guy is giving information on another important case."

Great, I thought, keeping the informant's identity secret was more important than my life.

"Don't worry, we will keep working this case hard, but we have to get you somewhere safe." Kent obviously had been delegated to deliver the bad news.

The U.S. Attorney added, "I've been in contact with Washington DOJ and the Bureau. They're sending up some relocation agents and working on a location."

"Relocation agents?"

Another agent working the case with Kent chimed in, "I think they're sending Gayle Wilson and Charles Nakada. They've been trained for this kind of thing."

The ASAC laughed, "Gayle Wilson, she used to be assigned up here, we called her the Gail Force. What a number, so serious and a real Bible thumper. Never heard of Nakada. What kind of name is that? Good luck."

No one else shared his good spirits, and the U.S. Attorney asked me to walk with him to his office.

I asked, "Any idea where they are going to put me until this blows over?"

"No idea. This is above my pay grade. The DOJ Criminal Division is talking to the Bureau."

I envisioned some Motel 6 located in Tulsa or Peoria. My experience had been that witnesses were usually relocated to some middling Midwestern city that was large enough for the witness to blend into without notice, but small and boring enough to discourage any tourism or interest. The shock of the day was wearing off, and an idea began to form. "Do you think I could make a suggestion?"

"Sure, let's do a conference call from my office."

On the phone were two men who, surprisingly enough, this lowly Assistant U.S. Attorney knew: the Assistant Attorney General in charge of the Department of Justice Criminal Division and the Director of the Federal Bureau of Investigation. Both had served as the United States Attorney for the District of Massachusetts during my prosecutorial career. They were Republicans with strong political ties, but they had happily endured this left-leaning prosecutor. The Director was a no-nonsense former Marine and decorated Viet Nam veteran who had tried some big cases; the head of the DOJ Criminal Division was a whip-sharp Harvard type whose family name adorned campus libraries.

I pictured these two men sitting in their comfortable D.C. offices, cradling phones, protected by layers of security, and enjoying their fireplaces. In Washington, it is the fireplace that defines the truly important Justice Department official. There are only four fireplaces within the massive Department of Justice structure, and they are reserved for the Attorney General, his deputy, and the heads of the Criminal and Civil Divisions. Within the more modern FBI headquarters, there is only one fireplace, the Director's. I felt a long way from the security or power of an office fireplace.

"What can we do to help?" asked the Director.

Well, I thought, things weren't all that bad if the Director of the FBI was taking my call and asking what he could do to help.

"How about relocating me to Yellowstone National Park until this gets resolved?" My boss looked profoundly puzzled. Snorting laughter came from the telephone conference speaker. I quickly explained my plan.

Instead of being squirreled away in some Midwestern motel, why not use an old Forest Service cabin nine miles up Slough Creek bordering the northeast corner of the Park? Little expense would be involved, no hired assassin would suspect such a hiding place, and I would be easy to protect in that isolated location. The Director had his qualms, but the Assistant Attorney General, a Yankee patrician who summered in remote Adirondack hideouts, chimed in with his full support, "Hey, you're always thinking. That's a great idea. Fly fishing on the federal dime. Why not?"

And so it was that I was flown, in complete secrecy and on a government plane, to Gardiner, Montana.

I met FBI Special Agents Nakada and Wilson at the private airstrip. Despite the early hour and strong wind, both agents looked remarkably put together. Being thirty-five, I judged each of them as easily five years younger and in substantially better physical shape. Charles Nakada was the first to hold out his hand. He was a model handsome mix of Japanese and American features with a strong chin, high cheek bones, and short, black hair. As he introduced himself, he displayed the easy confidence typical of FBI agents. It was reassuring to see him quickly scan the runway as he directed me toward his partner.

Gayle Wilson had the same serious attitude with a slightly upturned nose, dark hair attractively styled in a boyish cut, a solidly trim body, full lips, clear skin the color of milk chocolate, and a sawed-off shotgun. My kind of pretty when there is a contract on your head.

When I inquired about the weapon, Wilson responded in a light southern accent: "Charles is the marksman; he was a qualified sniper in the Army Rangers. But I sure get their attention up close with this." She softly tapped the barrel against her leg. I was feeling better.

"She just likes to show off with that bad boy," Charles added with a smile. These two obviously had been partners for a while and enjoyed a comfortable chemistry together.

We climbed into an impressive black Ford Expedition fully tricked out in law enforcement style. I briefed the agents on the details of the bank fraud investigation and the little I knew of the death threat. Gayle smiled when I finished, "Well, great balls of fire, you sure ticked some people off. I've never heard of white-collar crime types getting so upset."

"I guess I'm just lucky."

"Hey, we'll keep you safe enough if you follow directions." Then the female agent looked me over and added, "At least you're not one of those big macho drug prosecutor types."

When I said that I didn't know how to take this last comment, both agents laughed and Gayle steered us toward downtown Gardiner.

"I wonder why they chose Montana," Charles asked of no one in particular.

When I admitted that Montana was my choice, Gayle pulled to the curb, stopped, and turned toward the back seat, "You're kidding, right?"

As I looked out the tinted windows, I was reminded how down in the heels Gardiner always appeared. "It's much prettier up on Slough Creek."

Charles glumly added, "And I thought Fort Benning was bad."

Gayle chimed in with a pleasant drawl, "Well, you sure can't mistake this for South Carolina."

We were almost through town when I told them that we had to stop and pick up fishing gear. This required some effective advocacy on my part and the threat to call the Director. The mention of the Director turned the tide. Both agents reluctantly agreed that they did have access to the special account that permitted expenditures for relocating witnesses. In we went to Park's Fly Shop armed with a government credit card and numerous concealed weapons. As I explained the need for a fly rod, reel, line, leader, waders, and wading shoes, Gayle's southern hospitality appeared to fade. While I picked out numerous flies, she looked at the $600 price tag on the beautiful, deep green Winston fly rod, "Oh, yes, this will be easy to explain to the Director."

"Don't worry, he'll understand," I smiled and headed to the register.

Gayle pulled out the credit card and whispered to me, "This is definitely a white man's sport."

I was feeling better and better.

Negotiations at Yellowstone's Roosevelt Arch were not smooth. The Smokey Bear hat at the entrance was not expecting a display of official badges and an acknowledgment that we were fully armed. The Supervisor was called, explanations were given, and tempers cooled. The Supervisor assured us that horses were waiting for us at the Slough Creek trailhead, and we were off.

Yellowstone has the ability to impress even the most hardened law enforcement officer. Charles marveled at the elk strutting through the streets of Mammoth. Gayle pointed to the terraced hot springs spewing smoke into the cold autumn air. They were captivated by the buffalo herds near the Lamar and a lone wolf trotting up a steep hillside. Then came the horses.

Charles might have been a bad-ass Army Ranger, but his dapple-gray mount with the rolling eyes and stamping feet brought him down to my level. Neither of us felt comfortable climbing up on the distressingly lively Appaloosas provided by a very private dude ranch just north of the Park boundary. The Silver Tip Ranch was legendary because its ownership and guests were so secretive and wealthy, but I had no doubt that those gentlemen with the fireplaces had friends there. A weathered wrangler from the Silver Tip had packed the mules and informed us that we would each be leading a pack string. His laconic expression shifted only slightly as he looked again at Gayle. His light blue eyes narrowed to focus on an uncommon sight in Montana: an African-American woman slipping a shotgun into a rifle scabbard while giving orders. As the wrangler walked back to his pickup for a smoke, Charles and I looked at each other. Charles muttered, "Pack string?" and we shook our heads.

Then, Charles asked, "Why do they call it the Silver Tip?"

"It's another name for a grizzly." I added helpfully, "There are plenty of them up there."

"Oh, that's just great."

Gayle, by contrast, was in her element. She trotted around us as we tried to mount and offered encouragement mixed with laughter.

"Golly," she said, "I have to move my shoulder holster; it keeps hitting a rather sensitive place."

"They didn't teach you how to pack heat on a horse at Quantico?" I asked.

"Look counselor, just mount up and stay in the saddle or I can't protect you."

"Yes, ma'am."

"Now, that's more like it," she said, as she adjusted the shot gun in the leather scabbard and wedged the offending Glock under her belt. Her words were as firm as granite but her laugh was a delight.

The wrangler returned, the agents resumed their straight faces, and we headed north.

Gray clouds moved quickly against a hard-blue sky. The fourth meadow, nine miles up Slough Creek, was named Frenchy's Meadow after a French-Canadian poacher and trapper who loved the grassy clearing intersected by a winding stream and cupped by spruce-filled hills. Frenchy Duret died in this very meadow after he trapped, but failed to kill, a large grizzly. I gazed at his grave marker. It was the second headstone provided for the unlucky trapper. Reinforcing the fact that they stood on top of the food chain and were none too happy with the interloper, grizzlies tore up the first wooden marker honoring Frenchy. Another cloud blocked the sun, and the gravesite seemed to carry very bad ju-ju. A raven croaked nearby, and I wondered if my choice of location had been a serious mistake. More clouds gathered, the stream was discolored from a recent storm, and the Montana wind promised a cold night. I looked again at his marker; I did not want to join Frenchy.

I hauled my gear into the old Forest Ranger cabin festooned with the requisite elk antlers and bison skull. It was musty, dark, and filled with mouse droppings. After sweeping the place out, lighting the wood stove, cleaning out the lantern, and opening the shutters, it looked only slightly cozy. As darkness fell, I called Charles and

Gayle in from their canvas tent. They both looked discouraged and cold.

"Have you been to the outhouse yet?" Gayle asked.

"Is it grim?"

"All sorts of things must be living in there. I'm taking my shotgun with me next time."

"Christ," Charles added, "You freeze your butt out there."

The heat of the wood stove and the smell of the freeze-dried chicken stew seemed to help. I felt guilty being the cause of their discomfort. I opened a bottle of California cabernet provided, I suspected, by the Assistant Attorney General. When unpacking the panniers, I discovered the case with a note from the Cooke City Store that cheerfully and simply stated, "Tight Lines!" It was the type of thing a Harvard man, with a patrician sense of humor, might do. I poured the wine into three battered, semi-clean, enamel cups and toasted, "To warmer days and safe times." My companions dubiously raised their cups.

Gayle asked to say grace before we ate. She was sincere and serious. It set the tone for a quiet meal.

The next morning was not warmer. It was downright frigid. Gayle carried in her metal wash basin; it was frozen nearly solid and featured an ice bound mouse. "This, sir, is absolutely disgusting. What's for breakfast?"

I agreed with her assessment but could not resist adding, "Well, you can't mistake this for South Carolina." She huffed and we scrambled eggs on the cook stove.

The morning eventually became full of promise. By eleven, it was warm in the sun and I strung up the new fly rod. Charles was interested, but Gayle rolled her eyes as I explained attaching the leader, selecting the fly, and reading the water. Charles and I strolled down to Slough Creek. The stream was clearing nicely, and you could see an occasional large trout rise. I handed Charles my polarized sunglasses. He put them on and almost immediately expressed wonder, "Look, another one is coming to the surface!"

I cast a small foam beetle which was quickly swallowed by a fat cutthroat. The fish surged toward the bank, and I angled him out into the middle of the stream. When I brought him to hand, I showed Charles the orange slash and explained that the Yellowstone strain had this golden color with large black spots. Then I suggested that Charles take a cast. By this point, Gayle had long since abandoned us and was sitting next to her tent, face toward the sun, in some yoga pose.

I demonstrated the casting motion to my FBI student. When he initially took the rod back too far, I stood behind him and held his forearm when it extended beyond the one o'clock position. He took to it quickly. The fishing was easy and, after missing a couple of large slurping takes, he caught his first trout. It was the first time I had seen him smile. We took turns for the rest of the morning.

In the afternoon, I was handed over to Gayle.

I suggested we hike up the meadow.

"You don't want to fish?"

"Not unless you do."

"Let's hike."

The day was stunning. The sky was that clear autumn blue with a few white puffy clouds. The breeze was gentle and the tall meadow grass golden. Gayle halted on the lightly used trail, leaned back, flashed a big smile, and said, "God has smiled on this day."

I agreed, and we walked on. A small thermal stream emptied into Slough Creek and I reached down to feel the water. A little hotter than bathwater. I had a suspicion, and we hiked up the small stream. It led us uphill into the spruce. We clamored over deadfall and my hunch proved correct. In a small clearing we came to a good-sized thermal pool created by an impoundment of rocks and two smooth weathered logs.

Gayle had never seen such a pool.

"Is it safe?"

"It all depends on the temperature. It obviously has been made for bathing but let me check the water."

It was hot, but more than bearable.

"I'm going to soak," I announced.

"What are you going to do, just take off your clothes?"

"You got it."

She chuckled and turned away.

"This is great!"

"It's not too hot?"

"No, it's perfect. Come on in."

To my surprise, her response was, "Well, promise to God that you will close your eyes."

The promise was made and immediately broken.

She backed into the pool and I studied the small butterfly tattoo on the upper left corner of her beautiful butt. It was a sight worth remembering. I closed my eyes as she turned, adjusted herself, and declared, "Oh my Lord, this is heavenly."

I opened my eyes and looked at her smile. I was feeling better and better.

My right foot found her toes. She stiffened and said, "Look, no funny business here. Remember this Glock is right beside me." Sure enough, the handle was within her easy grasp. "It would be embarrassing to shoot the person I'm supposed to protect, but I could easily do it."

Then she smiled at my expression and added, "You couldn't handle my black ass anyway."

"Oh, I'm not so sure," I bravely replied. In truth, however, I was beginning to have my doubts as to whether I could handle, never mind satisfy, this lady.

"Seriously, I had my times when I was younger, but I'm born again and I mean it."

I did not doubt her for a minute.

After a quiet moment, she added, "Anyway, I'm here to protect, but not to serve." Her laugh cut all the tension.

We soaked, talked, and gazed up through the spruce to the blue heaven.

As we meandered back to camp, she asked "You really love it out here, don't you?"

I admitted that I did.

"Do you believe in God?"

I admitted that I did not.

"Do you think that all of this out here is your God?"

"It might be."

I pointed out a red-tailed hawk circling and giving its distinctive call.

"Whenever I see that sight, I think about what an old college professor quoted to me."

"And, what was that?" Gayle inquired.

"It's a poem that goes:

Why does the hawk wheel in the sky?

…he does it because he does it so well.

It is to praise God with his wings."

She turned and looked me in the face. "Boy, you might be a crazy. But you're a good man. I guess I'll have to protect that lily-white ass of yours."

"Lily-white ass? Now Gayle, how would you know? Did you peek?"

"Of course I did. Full knowledge is good for race relations."

I smiled, nodded, and asked, "Well, were you impressed?"

Again, that full-throated laugh, "Not at all."

We were nearly at camp when she broke a long, comfortable silence and asked, "Did you peek?"

It was the first time I had heard a slight shyness in her voice.

I confessed.

She raised her eyebrows, "Were you impressed?"

"Oh, mightily."

She gave another laugh, "Well, you darn well should be." Her usual tone was back.

The next day was a repeat of perfect weather. After a morning of chopping wood, cleaning, and checking the satellite phone for updates, Charles and I fished up to the thermal stream, caught plenty of cutthroats, and took a long soak. We walked back talking easily about work, books, and politics. He loved his job, was proud to be an agent, enjoyed biographies and crime thrillers, and, unlike many within the FBI, leaned toward the Democratic Party. I learned that he had attended Penn State on a ROTC scholarship, was a competitive target shooter, bike raced on weekends, and was still single. "As Joni Mitchell says, I'm busy being free." You have to like a former Army Ranger who quotes Joni Mitchell.

The sun was slanting sharply as we came within view of camp. Suddenly a large grizzly raised itself from the long grass, shook its massive head, and headed slowly in our direction.

Charles, who had never seen a grizzly, uttered "Holy Shit!" with a mixture of amazement and shock. He reached for his pistol, but the Glock seemed puny compared to this huge, lumbering beast.

Ranger and FBI training must not have covered bears, for Charles began to run and yelled, "Head for the river!" Old Frenchy could have told Charles that grizzlies are not deterred by a gentle trout stream and rather like the sight of fleeing prey. But flight seemed like a good enough idea at the time, and I was quickly on his heels.

Then I heard a loud crack and the earth below us disappeared. Suddenly there was a cloud of dust and debris around our heads and an overwhelmingly disgusting smell. When the cloud settled, I realized that we had run on top of an abandoned beaver lodge, crashed through, and were now trapped shoulder high as the bear confidently ambled our way.

The shattering blast followed. Gayle disappeared into the cabin to reload. The bear spun and spun again looking for the source of the noise. Then, with a loud huff, the grizzly lumbered off toward the line of spruce trees.

Charles hoisted himself out of the beaver lodge and helped pull me out. Battered and scratched, we ran to the cabin. Gayle opened the door.

"Good of you boys to return."

Charles bent over panting and responded, "I'm glad you didn't shoot us, partner."

"I wanted to blow a hole in that bear but shot over his head. I didn't want to deal with the National Park Service again."

"Good thinking," I wheezed.

Gayle opened the door and surveyed the meadow. When she saw it was empty, she shook her head, looked at me with a slight smile, and said, "I thought I was supposed to protect you from a contract killer, not bears."

That night we decided to all sleep in the log cabin. The canvas tent seemed no match for a grizzly, and I liked the idea of bunking with a lot of firepower.

I fished the morning hatch under gray, silent skies. Gayle studied me as I cast. She was looking forward to riding one of the Silver Tip's horses back to the trailhead and bringing in more food. I wished her well as a light drizzle started.

Charles and I surveyed our pitiful foodstuffs and decided to forgo lunch. I had found an old cribbage board and battered deck of cards in the cabin. Charles turned out to be a fast and fine cribbage player, and we finished five games by the light of the lantern.

I reached for the deck and said, "You're a good player. I think you win."

He covered my hand with his. I was surprised by the gesture and by the warmth and gentleness of his touch. His brown eyes held an intensity as he said, "You're good too."

Thinking back on it, I am surprised that I did not react more quickly or have some feeling of shock or revulsion. But I did not. His touch was pleasant, and he was so kind and sincere. He was a good man, and I did not want to hurt his feelings.

I slid my hand slowly away and said, "I'm awfully sorry."

Charles straightened in his chair, looked down quickly at his still extended hand, and blurted, "Oh, no, I am so sorry. I just thought.... I got the feeling. Well, I got the impression.... Oh, Christ, I am sorry. Please...."

"Hey," I interrupted, "There's nothing to it. Forget about it. Let's get the fire going before Gayle comes back."

"Yeah. But I was wrong. It wasn't appropriate. I'm so sorry."

"Hey, Charles, like I said, think nothing of it. It's just a mistake. No big deal."

"Oh, Christ on a crutch. I got it all wrong. I just have to go out for a walk and clear my head." And, with that, he left the cabin.

Charles didn't return until after Gayle showed up loaded with fresh steaks and baking potatoes. We bundled up, cooked the steaks on the outdoor grill, opened another bottle of wine, said grace, and ate like kings. But later, claiming that I snored too loudly, the agents went back to the canvas tent.

Charles made himself scarce after that. I fished different portions of Slough Creek, Gayle sat cross-legged on the bank meditating, and the cutthroat softly sipped ants, beetles, and blue winged olives.

After a day or so, I turned toward the golden bank and looked at Gayle. She was seated with her eyes closed, but I knew she was aware of everything. I asked, "Has Charles ever been married?"

Without opening her eyes, she responded, "No, and I suspect you know why."

"I guess I might."

She obviously was prepared for my question. In that light Southern accent she continued, "He's a real good man. God just made him different. You know we are all damaged goods in some way, but it's what we do in life that makes us holy. None of us knows how long we have on this earth. You should have learned that lesson this week. But, while we are here, we must try to make this world better. Charles definitely makes the world better."

I let my fly sink. "I know he's a good man. I just wish he wasn't trying to avoid me."

"He's afraid of you."

"Of me?"

She laughed softly and opened her eyes, "I know that's surprising, lily-white ass, but yeah, he's afraid of you. He knows you're close to the Director, and being gay will kick him out of the Bureau."

"But I would never tell."

"I know that, but he doesn't yet. Let me talk to him."

Gayle must have been good to her word because all was right again by dinner. We cooked, laughed, and enjoyed a beautiful sunset.

The call came early in the morning on the satellite phone. They had caught the hired gun. It was a routine traffic stop in Peabody, Massachusetts. He was pulling out of a strip club and forgot to turn on his headlights. The scoped rifle was in the back seat with its stock in plain view; he was a felon in possession and was quickly locked away on a parole violation. The crime boss who took out the hit was caught near Buffalo, New York. Before entering Canada, he had stopped to have a manicure and a pedicure. The FBI arrested him while his toes were soaking. After that, the bank president turned himself in. Charles related all of the news and concluded, "We always catch the dumb ones."

The satellite phone rang again. It was the Director checking in. I walked out of the cabin for privacy and praised Charles and Gayle at length. I told him that the FBI and the nation were lucky to have such fine agents. He agreed.

I was free to return. I felt almost light-headed with the news that no one was hunting me. I walked toward the creek. Somewhere on the spruce hillside, an elk was bugling loudly. The clear water moved silently, creating a surface of shifting currents. I felt relief but also a sorrow in leaving this place.

My return to Massachusetts didn't promise much. I was between girlfriends. There wasn't even a pet at home that would be happy to see me. Of course, I would check on my parents and tell stories to friends, but there was an undeniable emptiness. Charles and Gayle happily waved to me from the cabin. They couldn't wait to depart.

I waved back, told myself that I was being a self-absorbed prick, and turned my back on Slough Creek.

The Silver Tip promised to pack up our supplies, and, so, I reluctantly left the government-owned Winston fly rod and Abel reel with the sleeping gear, remaining food, and wine. Horses were saddled, and we headed south.

Charles and I walked our horses on the trail while Gayle cantered in wide circles swinging a straw cowboy hat she had liberated from the ranch. Without a pack string, we made good time. The trailhead was bristling with cars and trailers. Charles and Gayle were to backtrack to Gardiner and then fly to D.C. A Park Service ranger was waiting impatiently to drive me to a commercial flight from Jackson, Wyoming to Boston.

As we dismounted, Charles and I joked about sore knees and testicles.

Gayle gracefully swung off her saddle and handed the bridle to a wrangler. She turned to Charles and said, "Give me some cover for a couple of minutes, partner." Then, she led me behind the parked horse trailer.

She was like my sisters: younger but remarkably perceptive. Plus, she had that feminine ability to articulate feelings. "You're not looking forward to going back, are you?"

"Not much. I do love it here."

"God isn't just here. He's everywhere. Remember what I said. What we do in life makes us holy. We need good people like you. Go back to Boston and take care of the bad guys."

"Sort of like praising God with my wings?"

She gave a half laugh. "You got it, you God-denying lily ass."

"Thank you, Gayle, thank you for everything."

I smiled and turned to go. She took my elbow and gently turned me back toward her. Crooking a finger under my chin, she lifted slightly and stared. Her brown eyes were sprinkled with golden flecks.

"I saw a lot of you at that hot spring and a whole lot more out there in the wilderness. Everything, and I mean everything, impressed me."

She took a half step closer, and I was sure she was going to kiss me on the mouth. Instead, she gave a full smile, dropped her hand, and turned.

As she walked away, she gave a quick wiggle in her tight jeans.

After that, we talked every month or so. She always began each conversation with "Hi there, Lily." In typical FBI fashion, she had given me a codename. Often, it was worth the call just to hear her laugh. After a year, she fell out of touch and only occasionally returned my calls.

On another autumn day, almost two years after Slough Creek, Charles called. Gayle was very sick. It was pancreatic cancer. She had left D.C. months ago and was back home. She would not see anyone except Charles, her pastor, and her family. "Then, yesterday, she said she wanted to talk to you before hospice starts giving her morphine. I'm down here with her now."

Do not search for fairness in this world. Perhaps Frenchy deserved his death up in the meadow, but what of the Nez Perce families driven by the Army across the same ground? While these families slept, Howard and his companies fired Gatling guns and howitzers into the tepees of the tribe that, little more than a generation earlier, had fed, befriended, and saved the Corps of

Discovery as, the men starving, struggled across the Bitterroot Mountains. An old ER doctor reminded me of the same verity as he described a risky operation on a drunken child abuser, "No surprise, the operation was a shocking success. The bags of crap always survive, the rest of us die on the table."

In this frame of mind, I met Charles at the Columbia, South Carolina airport. Although neatly dressed and ramrod straight, he looked exhausted. We tightly hugged in the small terminal. "She's in bad shape." He tried to say something about Gayle being a partner, but his voice broke. He took a deep breath and looked away. Then he said in a hoarse voice, "I always loved her. Be prepared."

Two large black women looked up at me when I entered Gayle's room. As if confronting one of the four horsemen, they lowered their eyes, quickly rose from their chairs, and silently left.

In a very soft voice, Gayle said, "You scared them, Lily."

"I seem to do that to people."

"Yeah, I don't know why. I guess you're just too white."

She took an audible breath, patted the hospital bed, and said, "Come sit here."

She was barely recognizable. Her light chocolate skin had turned gray, her cheeks were hollow, and her lips had shrunken around her mouth. She took in another breath. "I'm sorry you have to see me this way."

"I'm so glad you let me come. I missed you."

She tried to laugh but only grunted. "Well, Lily, you'll miss me more soon. But I have made my peace with God, and I'm ready to go. In fact, I hope it comes soon."

WAY UP ON SLOUGH

I did not know what to say.

Gayle whispered, and I bent over to hear. Her breath was sour. "Remember that hot pool way up on that Slough Creek?"

"I'll never forget it. You looked great."

She moved and grimaced, "I sure hope heaven is like that."

"Only with a handsomer man."

This time she smiled.

"You better go up there again and catch one of those pretty fish for me."

"Oh," I replied, "I probably will."

"No, promise me. You are so happy up there. Promise me you will, for me."

"I promise, Gayle."

"Good. You've got to go now. I'm getting tired. Give me a kiss."

I did and remembered to add, "Everything about you impresses me."

She closed her eyes, patted my hand, and whispered, "Do good. And, look for me when you're up on that creek. I'll be there."

Chapter Nine: *A Hole You Never Fill*

A sinking ship in a dark sea leaves a wake of horror and emptiness. I hold my father's hand and he gives the slightest squeeze goodbye. I assure him that I will be right back. Despite what is diagnosed as a brain aneurysm, I know he understands. I explain that I just need to take a quick shower and change the clothes I threw on this morning after he called. When I return, he no longer understands. Soon the irregular beat turns into a flat line and the nurse, head down, quietly turns off the monitor.

How can this happen to a loving, witty, intelligent father of five children, to a cherished college professor on the day of his happily anticipated retirement, to a modest war hero who left college, joined the Army as a private, and survived the bloody Pacific island-hopping, to a sixty-five-year-old man who was just recovering his spirits after two years of grieving the loss of his younger wife? I cannot begin to think of answering the unanswerable. I can only mindlessly plod through funeral details and, then, leave. Nothing is fair; nothing makes sense.

I do not grieve by crying or reminiscing. I simply take a plane from Boston to Idaho. I flee. I escape. I try to keep my mind blank, but I cannot forget that slight squeeze of goodbye.

I made my way to my small cabin in Pierre's Hole, Idaho where one can still find the wild, romantic beauty about which historian Bernard DeVoto rhapsodized. Lush barley and potato fields border the peaceful spring creek that bisects the valley. To the west lie the Big Hole Mountains, and to the east the spectacular Tetons loom above the foothills. It is no wonder that Jeddediah Smith, the

Sublettes, and the rest of the early mountain men decided to hold their most famous summer rendezvous on this side of the Tetons.

But the last thing I wanted was quiet reflection in the shadow of the Teton peaks. I needed to keep moving; the massive stands of cedar, spruce, and fir of northern Idaho beckoned. Mary Kate, my long-time, if fading, girlfriend called, to subtly check on my mental state. She listened with quiet concern when I told her that I was leaving immediately for a long road trip. After a few difficult moments, she wished me a safe voyage. Always one with a streak of religion, she added, "I'll pray for you, and I've asked God to kiss you on the forehead."

If only I possessed this Catholic girl's comforting belief. She knew that I am cut from a more agnostic cloth, and she simply sighed when I tried to present a brave, frivolous front by responding that I hoped that I would not need too much divine guidance to capture eager west slope cutthroat trout. With her benediction, I loaded my rental car and headed for the panhandle.

My drive began in the dreary lava beds of southern Idaho—my mood matching the dark craggy vista. I was glad to escape the pocked rock slabs and reach the small town of Mud Lake, Idaho. Slowing to thirty miles per hour, I looked at a street front fit for Edward Hopper: a farm implement showroom, an abandoned grocery store, and a bar. Mud Lake, the name said it all. This was followed by dull miles of sage brush, "no trespassing" signs, and barb-wired nuclear reactors. Welcome to the federal government's National Engineering Laboratory. The blue highway signs chirped "Quality People Doing Quality Research." Thoughts of hazardous nuclear waste and government minions pressed my foot to the gas pedal.

A HOLE YOU NEVER FILL

The scenery improved as I coasted through the lonely Lemhi Valley. I felt lucky to find a gas station that sold candy bars on this two-hundred-mile stretch. Children who grew up in the now nearly abandoned downs of Lone Pine, Hahn, and Gilmore must have been overjoyed to leave these windy, barren hills behind. I felt the heavy weight of depression and scanned the dial for an upbeat song. No radio station reached the depths of the Lemhi.

Dropping into the lush Bitterroot Valley of Montana was a startling contrast to the quiet, Mormon-dominated confines of eastern Idaho. The bars proudly advertised two-for-one drinks, dancing, poker, and who knows what else. It sounded rather tempting, but it was only early afternoon.

Because no roads travel north through the incredibly rugged mountains of northern Idaho, one must detour through Montana to reach the Idaho panhandle. My goal was the neat, modest town of Superior, Montana. Superior, labeled a "city" by Montana standards, seemed frozen in the Eisenhower administration. Mary Kate and I had discovered an excellent café here while repairing a tire during an earlier camping trip. Fortunately, from my point of view, she had run out of clean bras and was bouncing about in a T-shirt as we entered the café. This sight raised a few Stetsons and ball caps at the counter, and Mary Kate, blushing, whispered, "They all must think I'm some Mountain Mama. Let's sit down quickly."

I smiled at the memory of Mary Kate with her dancing brown eyes, frequent smile, and round cheeks. I had met her while recovering from a romantic disaster. A beautiful girlfriend had chosen an up-and-coming doctor over me; you can't always get what you want. The breakup was hard on me, but not on her. It set me adrift.

Mary Kate's constant good nature, grounded attitude and simple wholesomeness were a welcome relief. We loved hiking into the Idaho wilderness together to fish and camp along the rivers and creeks. In winter, she taught me how to ski the deep powder of western mountains. We enjoyed three very good years together, and now we were concluding a rocky fourth. We cared for each other deeply, but knew that there was something missing. Or, at least, we thought there was. In the end, we squandered what we had. She was, secretly, but not so secretly, beginning to date another man who I vaguely knew. He was a fine guy, and I truly hoped she found complete happiness. We did not talk of parting, but knew we soon would. It was a mistake revisiting this café. I took a sip of the regionally weak coffee and left.

There is a pleasure in turning off a highway and onto a gravel road. My atlas assured me that this was the forest road that led to Hoodoo Pass and back into the wilds of Idaho. The road over Hoodoo Pass is a white-knuckle affair winding up a tall mountain without a hint of a guard rail. The logging trucks that barrel down the road raise enough dust to blind any driver within a half mile. Prayer may be the best approach. A prayer that you do not meet one of these lumbering beasts speeding around a tight corner, for destruction is certain.

At ten o'clock, the nearly endless daylight of a northern Idaho summer was beginning to wane as I pulled into the Kelly Creek campground. The campground, hardly a slice of wilderness beauty, consisted of a series of randomly placed fire rings, a few pick-up trucks and horse trailers strewn about a meadow, and a fair amount of horse manure. It all looked fine to my travel-weary bones, and I happily pitched a tent and started a fire. A mule deer roamed the overlooking hill, stopped, and stared at me.

A HOLE YOU NEVER FILL

After replacing the ever-fractured mantles on my Coleman lantern, I hustled into my well-worn sleeping bag with an aluminum cup of sixteen-year-old Scotch and a hook-and-bullet article about this very creek. Kelly Creek is nearly famous, made so by the fly-fishing heavyweights—people who fish throughout the world and actually make some sort of living by writing about fish, flies, and tackle. I find such kiss-and-tell pieces unsettling and vaguely immoral, and I read them avidly. This magazine article stuck to the formula and described the deep-bodied cutthroats striking various attractor patterns with abandon. I read by the light of the wheezing old Coleman about how the air sparked while the water rushed clean and clear, and how the writer escaped the twentieth century by fly fishing on this empty, wilderness stream. The prose certainly did not equal Maclean's, but it was enough to get the adrenalin running in this armchair angler. Finally, I dozed off on my hard foam mattress, exhausted.

Someone cranked up a generator. The sky was still a dawn gray. The sun wouldn't shine into the canyon for hours. I lolled about in my sleeping bag not wanting to face the cold dew and wondered how heavy my pack was going to feel. The hike to my preferred camping spot was only about four miles, but I never had prided myself on being a pack horse.

I crouched down and hoisted the pack on my back. It felt punishingly heavy, much heavier than the last time I made this trip. And, of course, it was. The last time I hiked this stretch was with Mary Kate. A generous and strong woman, she cheerfully split the load. I felt no aching loneliness without her, but I now missed her good humor and strong back. As I trudged toward the trail, a black tail doe near the trail head stopped her grazing to look up at this sorry sight; she seemed unburdened.

I started at a fast clip, but soon my pace dropped off until I was simply putting one foot in front of the other. My mind began to wander. I likened myself to Nick Adams hiking off to find solitude and solace along a trout stream after confronting the shattering experience of death. The thought helped for about the first two miles. Thereafter, I focused on the spectacular scenery of green hills, rocky cliffs, spruce towering against wide skies, shallow riffles and deeper blue pools. This was the land of the Big Burn of 1910 when hurricane-force winds concentrated numerous wildfires into a fireball that burned an area the size of Connecticut. The blackened snags still stand like sentinels over and among the spruce and underbrush.

Finally, I rounded a corner and spied my destination. You could not miss it, a beautiful grove of fir and ferns where Cayuse Creek meets the Kelly. I bounced down the hillside from the high trail and confronted four hobbled llamas resting placidly among the waist-high ferns. This was a surprise. Closer inspection revealed a bevy of family members pitching three tents on the far side of the grove. Luckily, the grove was large and the llamas remarkably quiet. I slunk over to an unoccupied clearing hard by the creek.

There is a solace in setting up a camp. I snapped the tent poles together, stretched the nylon fly and staked it down, and rolled out the sleeping bag. No matter what happens now, I thought, I have a safe harbor.

Next, I turned to my fishing gear and fit the smooth, lustrous rod pieces together. With the simple black reel screwed into the silver holder at the rod's base and the heavy peach-colored fly line strung through the guides, I proceeded to tie on the light monofilament leader, then selected a fly and tied it onto the leader's end. The rigged rod was beautiful. I leaned back against a large cedar, closed my eyes, and listened to the creek.

Heading upstream, unburdened by my pack, I felt light, almost free. Above Cayuse, long stretches of Kelly Creek are too shallow to hold good-sized fish. I wanted to concentrate on the deeper pockets and pools where the creek enters a deep, boulder-filled canyon. In the past, I had enjoyed great success in these pools drifting hopper patterns and getting strike after strike. After a mile, I reached the first promising spot. I quickly angled down from the path onto the bank. I cast. My hopper pattern, a slim combination of deer hair and pheasant feathers tied by my friend Jack, drifted downstream untouched. This was puzzling. It was prime hopper time, eleven in the morning. There was a nice breeze and plenty of hoppers danced about the bank vegetation. But as Jack always told me, cast and keep moving. I went around the bend to the next pool.

There, to my further surprise, was someone whipping a fly line around. This was not the solitude I had expected. I joined the hoppers and clambered up the bank so as not to disturb my competition. No problem, I consoled myself, I will simply hike up a few bends and out distance this fellow. Still, I could not remember Nick Adams being disturbed by anyone as he fished in Michigan's Upper Peninsula.

As I hiked by, I glanced over at my competition and gave a most insincere smile and wave. Who was this bird? Adorned with a floppy white canvas hat, he was casting enthusiastically, if not expertly, while still wearing his hiking boots and fully loaded backpack.

He was a cheerful, even exuberant fellow. "Only small ones so far, how about you?" The accent seemed to beckon more from

Appalachia than Idaho. With the floppy hat and an aged pack that sprouted cups, plastic bags, and some tattered clothing, he resembled a vagrant panhandling for spare change on an urban street.

Before I had a chance to respond, he happily continued, "What'cha using? Every time I fish, I try 'em all, but I think I'd do just as good if I stuck with the renegade."

Since using the simple renegade fly pattern is nearly a religious requirement within the working class of Idaho—it is frequently derided by high-priced fishing guides as a "farmer fly" —I decided that perhaps this fellow did hail from the Gem State.

I attempted to avoid answering his first question by answering the second. "I've been using a hopper pattern."

Although I did not consider my comment particularly witty, this guy laughed heartily, "I was using the same damn thing right below here and didn't catch nothing."

I wished him good luck and quickly hiked another half mile up the trail.

A riffle emptied into a modestly deep pool, and the current gently swept by a large boulder on the far bank—the stuff of Boston daydreams. This was a perfect cutthroat pool, deep enough to hold good fish but not so deep as to make them uninterested in feeding on the surface. Those chubby trout could wait in the steady current for the food bouncing down the shallow riffle. Even better, a few smaller fish were dimpling the pool. Confidence regained, I cast through the foot of the pool. Still, no interest in the hopper.

I searched the water's surface for any hatching insect. Nothing. I concluded, once again, that this "match the hatch" technique, so popular among the famed fly fishers, was highly overrated. Out of deference to Idaho, I clipped off the hopper and rummaged about for a fly named the "sterling trude." It is a peculiar fly created down on the Henry's Fork in southeastern Idaho with a white wing and a bright red bottom. Its colorful rump reminded me of a baboon, and, for that reason, I liked it.

Proving the odd nature of fishing, my first cast caught a ten-inch cutthroat. "Like I told you, they all seem small up here!" I quickly turned. There he was again, on the bank, smiling broadly, crooked bottom teeth, pack fully loaded, and worn hiking boots dripping wet. How did this bird travel so fast? "Looks like a good pool you got there." "I hope so," I replied, as cheerfully as possible.

I cast toward the middle of the pool. A beautiful long, fat westslope cutthroat slowly rolled over the trude and put up a dogged fight, running well downstream and stripping line from the reel. This was a hefty fish for such a creek. My companion and I agreed upon the beauty of the fish. He was certainly in a good position to judge because he was now leaning over my shoulder as I removed the fly from the fish's jaw.

"Let me see what'cha using." After examining the trude, he hopped up onto the bank and was off again.

The pool brought a few more trout, and I felt satisfied as I waded around the bend.

I rather expected to find him at the next pool, so I waved, this time a bit more sincerely, and headed along the trail into the canyon. Three hundred yards later I decided to drop down into the last of the easily accessible canyon pools. It was a beauty: massive boulders and green swirling water. "Hello there," a voice called from under my foot.

"My god," I mumbled as I jumped back. I had nearly stepped on this guy as he sat eating a peanut butter sandwich in the dark shade of one of the huge boulders. How did this guy travel so fast with that pack? He reminded me of Marley's ghost who, though fettered by chains and cashboxes, traveled endlessly on the wings of the wind. I briefly debated whether I should mention this allusion to Dickens, but he spoke first.

"Go ahead and fish this spot. I'm eating lunch."

I unartfully lied, "Oh no, I just wanted to look it over. I'm going back for lunch now anyway." What moron, I wondered, would believe such a line?

"Where," I asked, "are you going to camp?" I wanted to pin down this distraction.

"Well, I just don't know, up along a ways, I suppose." He smiled before taking another bite of the sandwich.

As I walked back to camp, I still felt fully rooted in the late twentieth century. Nick Adams, I thought, where are you?

The grandfather of the neighboring family clan was standing beside my tent on his way to feed the llamas. We made small talk about a llama's diet, its habits, and its ability to pack heavy loads. Perhaps Grandpa was as bored with the conversation as I was because he suddenly stopped and asked, "So you're camping out here all by yourself?"

"That's right," I replied, probably with a bit of pride and irritation seeping into my voice.

He looked around at my one-man tent, the small camp stove, and solitary pack and shook his head slightly. Without a word he moved off toward his llamas.

The afternoon was hot. I stretched out and slept under the magnificent cedar that shaded my camp. I awoke as late afternoon thunder rolled through the valley. The llamas had hopped nearer to my tent. At this closer range, they looked rather sweet and dumb. They reminded me of a kind-hearted, mentally challenged, girl I knew in the fourth grade. I stood and slowly approached both the llamas and my tent. Although I was still a full five feet away from the seemingly sweet, dim-witted animals, the closest llama twisted its neck quickly, curled back its lips in a grotesque smile, and vomited foul-smelling, greenish-yellow snot on my left shoulder and arm.

As I sat in a small pool, scrubbing my arm and neck with river sand while wringing out my shirt, I looked up at the dark cumulous clouds that had filled the sky and listened to the busy water of the creek. Facing the wilderness and with the stream shielding any sound, I began to cry. Of course, there was no rational basis for this drama. Here I was a man well into his thirties, a successful hard-nosed federal prosecutor, with enough money to jet out to the wilds of Idaho and fly fish. A man with excellent health, whose father had lived a full life. Of course, I wept all the more. Finally, I lay face first in the stream and dunked my head toward the stony bottom, then stood up, pushed the hair out of my face, and headed to shore.

I grabbed some beef jerky and laid a small fire for the late evening. As I crumpled paper and broke kindling, I noticed that the fire ring was filled with well burnt cans. All part of camping in the late twentieth century.

I fished into the long twilight of a northern Idaho summer evening. Wading in shorts and sneakers from one run to the next, I made short casts and watched my caddis imitation drift like a miniature sail down the golden, glassy runs. By nine-thirty I worked my way back to camp. The driftwood was dry and the fire crackled in the darkness. I sipped warm whiskey from my metal cup and thought of the Highland Scots who enjoyed the same endless summer days and frowned on anyone who dared dilute the malt with ice cubes.

I was out of my tent before the sun kissed the canyon walls, planning to hike upstream to the Hanson Meadows. If I waited until the sun was up, the six-mile hike would turn brutally hot. Water bottle and wading shoes strapped to my belt and wearing a fishing vest, I walked quickly to warm myself on this frosty morning. The cold numbed my hands. I opened and closed both the left and right, making fists and switching the rod case from one hand to the other. After two miles, all the cold had left me.

I kept a close eye out for that bird with the white floppy hat and the backpack. Where did he camp? What if he was already at the Meadows dredging every pool? I searched every clearing for the sign of his camp and, relieved, found nothing.

Halfway through the hike, I skirted a bog and startled a cow moose and a black tail doe. The moose lumbered off with a hurried, awkward trot, but the doe moved but a few steps, turned back and watched me climb another ridge. Around the next corner a mule deer buck looked up from the trail and effortlessly hopped off in a series of high, arching leaps through the deadfall. By this point, I was beginning to believe that the deer had kissed me on the forehead and were watching over me.

At the cliff overlooking Hanson Meadows, I regretted my lack of a camera. The creek wound through the boggy meadows like a crystal thread, and the backdrop was uninterrupted, endless fir and pine. There was no sign of another living soul. I thanked God that I was alive and lucky enough to see such places.

A HOLE YOU NEVER FILL

My earlier fears proved groundless. The floppy white hat was not in the Meadows. Only the Clark's nutcrackers flew noisily from tree to tree. Along a deep run next to the bank, I hauled out four good-sized cutthroats.

The creek turned sharply at the end of the Meadows into a forest thick with deadfall and overhanging firs that nearly touched the water. Hoisting myself over a large dead Douglas fir, I worked my way into the tangled darkness. Ahead of me, several small riffles hit the side of a cliff, joined and then fell into the loveliest pool I had ever seen. Trout were rising near the head of the pool. Far from some tangled, tragic swamp, this was paradise.

Having carefully crossed the creek to a small sandy beach below the towering firs, I roll-cast a small parachute Adams into the tail of the pool. The shade was so deep that I could only guess the fly's location. A trout smacked the fly with such a flourish that even a blind man would know to set the hook. A fat westslope cutthroat bulled around the pool, making run after run. More finely spotted trout with green backs, brilliant orange slashes, and full bellies splashed with red spawning colors came to the small fly. I worked the pool for many fish, releasing each back into the liquid emerald. As I reached the riffles that formed the head of the pool, I shouted my joy.

Afterwards, I sat in the meadow, watching two red-tailed hawks circle in the endless blue Idaho sky, and prepared my legs for the hike back. I savored the feeling of the sun on my face and the memory of the trout. The llamas, with their green snot and curled lips, seemed far away. The trail climbed steeply out of the meadow. Head down, I put my legs into the task.

I looked up when I heard branches breaking. I first saw the floppy white hat, then the stuffed backpack, and then the wide smile. "Looked like you were having fun at that pool," he cried as he hopped onto the trail. "I was up on the hillside glassing for elk, and I saw you down in the meadow."

I caught my breath. "Yeah, the fishing was good."

"I thought it would be," he happily responded. "I camped up here in the meadow but left that last pool for you. I was thinking you'd come on up."

I was slightly stunned by his childlike, unfiltered enthusiasm and true kindness. I looked closely at his weathered face for the first time. Despite the whiskers, the dirt, and the large reddish nose, there was a softness to the face, and his clear green eyes sparkled like cool, clear pools.

"Well, I got to get back up that ridge." He turned and headed back through the thick brush and up the steep slope.

"Thank you," I called. Without turning, he raised his right hand in acknowledgment and was swallowed by the small pines and bushes. He moved almost as smoothly and quickly as the mule deer.

A mile from camp, I decided to fish the pool at the end of the canyon. This time, no one was lunching in the shadows of the boulders. I scrambled down and cast from behind a huge rock. A trout slowly drifted up and sucked down the fly. It was the largest of the trip. I placed the spawning male against my rod and saw that he was close to twenty inches. I looked around, hoping in some way that the white floppy hat had materialized so that I could share this incredible fish with him. But it was only me, and the water, and the rocks. I slid the fish into the pool.

The llamas were gone when I returned to camp. The family had left. I was alone at the junction of two wilderness streams.

A HOLE YOU NEVER FILL

The next morning I plucked at least a dozen burnt cans from the fire ring and shoved them into my old pack. It was the least I could do in return.

I expected the hike out to seem shorter than the hike in, but the opposite was true. Repeatedly I assured myself that the trailhead was around the next bend, only to realize that it was still far off as I rounded that bend and gazed ahead. I stretched my back and then scanned the scenery and the changing shadows on the hillsides. Heading up the final incline, I saw a mule deer nodding at me and staring off in the direction of the road as if guiding me home.

Chapter Ten: *Memorial Day*

It is late May—Memorial Day, in fact—and the heat finally has come. The peepers have surrendered to the crickets. The windows are open, and only a sheet covers me. Having botched another love affair, I have all night to burn. She used to nestle her blonde head on my shoulder, her arm draped over my chest, and her soft breathing would put me to sleep. We fit so well together that I was half convinced that she was the one. I think these thoughts at odd night hours during this latest romantic hiatus. In order to escape thinking, I eagerly rise at one, two, or three in the morning depending upon the demands of the tide chart.

We just didn't reach that next level of commitment or comfort or security. She fixed me with her pale blue eyes and, in her Norwegian accent, accused me of not trying. I blamed her for leaving and cursed my luck. At the end of a relationship, it is the good, the bad, the lazy, and the scared. The difficulty is in figuring out who qualifies for which title. I don't relish these memories or the suspicion that I have become one of those jerks who push a female aside for some selfish whim or desire as though love was disposable and a replacement easily obtained at the next corner.

I reflexively layer myself with shirts and then a sweater. It is never warm waist deep where the river meets the sea. The tide is falling along the great stretch of mud and marsh known as Joppa Flat. I pull on my waders and start across the black flat. It is dark as ink, but the light fog does not hide the stars or the slow green blinking of the buoy lights.

I slog at a diagonal to just miss the moored boats, toward the river's mouth. The massive current sweeps stronger there, and that is where the bigger bass will be feeding. The mud sucks at my boots as if trying to hold me back. After 200 yards of this, I am breathing hard. If she saw me now, she would tip her head back and let out that throaty laugh. Hair rumpled, smelling of insect repellant, out in the middle of the mud on a black night and up to my hips in the water, cripes, I think to myself, what an existence: sleep in the day, out in the dark water most every night. I'm a real catch. No wonder she left. But I know it is not that simple.

As I walk the next hundred yards, I hit tiny swirling algae that light up as I splash through them. Sparks of greenish white phosphorescence swirl around me as though the stars had fallen under the water. I am near my destination. There are other fishermen out on the flat. I can barely see the closest one but hear the rest. They stand waist deep in a ragged, curving line starting at the moored boats.

Most are close enough to each other to carry on a limited conversation of what flies or retrieves they are trying. They seem to be in pairs, fishing partners who keep up a steady line of talk, punctuated by excitement when they feel a tug on their line.

Spurred by this competition, I wade out farther and deeper. The school of bass are all about, and I hear the occasional straining of a reel against the light lapping of water and knocking of masts. It is a happy bunch back near the moored boats. The schoolies are cooperative, hitting most any fly pattern and laughter occasionally rolls out into the darkness.

I work my way toward the mouth of the river and away from the pack. I am up to my chest and feel the current's strong pull; I back a few steps, strip out line and cast. It isn't pretty—just pitching the fly out as far as I am able, slowing stripping in the line, and peering beyond the rod into the darkness to see if a fish boils as the steamer slowly swings through the end of the retrieve. This is not a sport of quiet contemplation out here in the strong dark current hoping for a fish larger than my thigh to attack. I feel my shoulders and neck tense as I follow the course of the fly. The salt water stings the line burns and cracks in my right hand.

A fish hits. It is a schoolie, and I horse it in quickly and try to release it before it splashes and attracts attention. The last thing I want is for the happy duos to collect down here.

I look up river, about thirty yards, to the one fisher close enough to see. I am both irritated and reassured by the company; the fewer people stirring in the water, the better. But on a moonless night, some distant human companionship is welcome when one confronts the eerie combination of the oily black rushing water and the current's deep tug. I was on the flat last night only to have a large seal's head rise two feet in front of me while I was chest deep and hooked onto a striper. I felt a jolt of fear at suddenly looking into those large watery eyes.

The fellow well upriver has a fish. He lets out a whoop of genuine happiness and begins reeling in line. He yells to the stars,"This is a great country." I smile at this shouted observation and cast again.

I hear his fish slapping on the surface. He certainly is not trying to unhook the fish quietly and keep his luck a secret. "This is beautiful! Where can you do this but in the U.S. of A!"

The patriotic outburst makes me turn upstream, and I miss a strike. Perhaps the Memorial Day weekend has stirred the man's passions. Maybe he still sings "The Star Spangled Banner" out loud at ball games.

Only a minute passes before the next yell, "Another! This is great! You commies don't have fishing like this."

This fellow's ongoing broadcast in the dark is like listening to the Voice of America. Does he understand that the iron curtain collapsed in a heap of rust years ago? A heavy strike jars me back to reality. I set the hook and the fish heads straight out. I cannot turn him, and he is in the current. The thick fly line burns off the reel and I am quickly into the backing. The thin backing line hums smoothly off the spool as the fish runs. Luckily, striped bass are basically lazy, and this fish finally stops and bulls in and out for a good while. "I love to hear the music of the drag. You're playing my song." The super patriot suddenly materializes next to me. The seal would be more welcome.

At last I bring in this fish. It is a beauty. We both stare at the big silver-striped sides glistening in the darkness. I am pleased, but not as much as my newfound companion. He shouts out into the current, "You don't have fish like this, you fucking Red Chinese!"

I expect to see a Sylvester Stallone or Arnold Schwarzenegger type, but it is only a slight, balding fellow who is shipping water as it laps over his waders. He is obviously comfortable in his time warp where good and evil are easy to proclaim.

"Jesus, it's deep. I've got to step back here." It is interesting how water tricking down one's belly and leg can cool the passions of the most ardent defender of the American way. Back he steps and just stands there, rod under his arm, watching me.

What the hell. I cast, slowing stripping the large black fly so that it sinks and darts into the water. A big swirl, and I know it is another good fish.

"Yes, yes, yes! Take that, you suicide-bombing bastards! Take that god damn Saddam!" The man has no trouble jumping from one generation, ideology or continent to another.

MEMORIAL DAY

I have little time to listen to the vitriolic tirade behind me. I am trying to make sure the line is smoothly coming off the reel as I try to urge the fish to run toward shore.

"Take that, Al-Qaida! You got no fish in your crappy desert!"

The man is shouting at the top of his lungs in the middle of a mud flat, in the dead of night, with current surging about his waist. Oddly his excitement is contagious.

It is a great fish. She runs again and again. I feel giddy. Maybe it is the excitement of the fish, maybe the phase of the moon, maybe some subliminal purging of youthful protest marches. I join in: "Take that, Uncle Ho!" "Yeah," my companion echoes, "Take that, Uncle Ho fucking Chi Minh!"

We are both shouting. The fish surges again, the reel's drag reaches a high pitch. I am completely caught up in the spirit, "Ever hear that song, Osama?"

"Yeah! God damn Osama bin Laden, ever catch fish like this? Bring him home brother!"

The big striper is finally exhausted, pressed between my arm and hip. My hands are shaking. He is clapping me on the back and calling me "my man" and "soldier." I grab the lower jaw, unhook the fish, and she slowly drifts away with the current. The bass leaves a bright phosphorescent wake almost as a gift. We stand shoulder to shoulder for a full minute staring into the dark. I clip the fly off my line and hand it to this fellow.

"Here, they seem to like this pattern tonight."

"What? You're going in? This tide is still good."

My teeth are beginning to chatter. "Yeah, I'm going in. I 've been out too deep for far too long." I start slogging for the shore. A few minutes pass, and I hear a familiar shout, muffled only slightly by distance.

"This is beautiful! Castro! Ever catch a striper? I'm talking to you Fidel, you son of a bitch! This is the U.S. of A."

I head straight for shore, although I cannot see it yet. Daybreak will not come for another hour.

Chapter Eleven: *This Your Rig?*

I scan this flat, Western mountain valley lying beneath a brutally hot blue sky. Our truck has disappeared. My Eastern mind jumps to various nefarious conclusions, but the possibility of theft in this rural Mormon stronghold is nil. I look again. It can't be far; I'd only been in the trailer-sized convenience store for a minute. I hear before I see: "This your rig?"

I turn. Three hundred yards away, down an imperceptible slope, the rented truck rests hard against the only other man-made object in sight—a tiny cabin that appears constructed of plywood. This Rent-a-Wreck product obviously popped gears and rolled, as if lonely or magnetically attracted, to the only other manufactured object in this sagebrush setting.

A large fellow with one overall strap covering a hairy chest is sipping a cup of coffee and observing the pickup with cracked windshield crushing his flower bed and nudging the corner of his home. I arrive out of breath and ill prepared for the traditional showdown involving the exchange of accusations and insurance information.

He takes another sip of coffee and repeats, "This your rig?"

I fully acknowledge ownership and ask the obvious, "Is this your house?"

"You bet," he responds in that slow soft tone that seeps into the American tongue west of the Mississippi. "The wife and I were having coffee and wondered who was coming to visit. Then we wondered if they'd stop. They didn't. This here truck just kept right on coming."

"Look, I am awfully sorry." My tone is not soft and my pace not slow. "Let me give you my name and address and registration."

"Don't worry now. It looks like your rig got the worst of the deal." Sure enough, the left headlight and bumper are well bruised and the tiny cabin miraculously shows not a nick.

"Sorry it's under these circumstances, but it's nice to meet you. What's your name?" and my overall-clad companion extends a big muscular hand.

After further talk and inspection of my rig, I back out of the small patch of zinnias bordering the cabin. He lightly taps the roof of the cab, wishes me well and offers a piece of advice. "You best keep a tight rein on this outfit."

This was not the optimal beginning of a belated honeymoon. Jessica and I were six months married, and I had spurned friends' suggestions to relax at various fancy Western dude ranches. Instead, I decided to take my new bride on the most fascinating portion of the Lewis and Clark trail. This was well before the much ballyhooed two hundredth anniversary celebration, and few travelers enjoyed the splendor of this mountainous corner where Lewis first crossed the Continental Divide in search of the Northwest Passage.

After the collision with the small cabin, Jess inquired if it would be wise to return to the big city of Idaho Falls and exchange vehicles. I quoted the most used phrase penned by William Clark and Meriwether Lewis in their famous journal, "We proceed onward." So, the battered, noisy pick up—like an aging bull with a crumpled horn—headed north into Idaho's Lemhi Valley.

Jess graced this trip with considerable charm and civilization. This stood in marked contrast to my past Western rambles. Gone were the Cheez Whiz and saltines; we stocked the cooler with brie, celery sticks, and Perrier. She also stuffed a variety of Western guidebooks and histories into the glove box to ensure that this trip did not degenerate into a single-minded search for trout. As we rolled along the willow-lined Lemhi River, she read that near here Meriwether Lewis, having survived the rigors of pulling a barge against the raging Missouri and marching across three thousand miles of wilderness, finally reached the long-promised point where the waters began to flow toward the Pacific. He was the first white American to invade this wilderness and, Jess, with a touch of surprise, observed that Lewis accomplished this precisely one hundred and ninety years ago: August 12, 1805.

All the sketchy maps and information of the day assured Lewis that it would now be a quick downstream trip to the Pacific. Reaching the crest, he noticed the waters running west, knelt, cupped his hands, and later wrote, "Here I first tasted the water of the great Columbia river." Then he looked out with great anticipation. He did not see the hoped-for Columbia or even a steady decline toward the west. There was no fabled Northwest Passage. Instead, the mentally unsteady Lewis had to deal with the most discouraging of sights: an endless series of jagged "immense" peaks with their "tops partially covered with snow" ranging westward to the horizon. This was foreign land, completely unlike the gentle, rounded slopes of the familiar Blue Ridge and Appalachians. Perhaps Jess was channeling Lewis's thoughts when she studied the desolate valley and the rearing mountains, "My god, how does anyone live here?"

I have taken my bride to this part of the country which always has given me the most wonderful of times and memories. After all, this is the same Lemhi Valley where the expedition's indispensable guide, Sacagawea, found happiness. As you may recall, Sacagawea, as a six-year-old girl, was kidnaped from this area, traded to the Mandan tribe, and married off to a lazy French-Canadian trapper in present-day Missouri. After enduring this grim life, it was here that she enjoyed a miraculous family reunion. Lewis and Clark, desperate for horses and reliant on Sacagawea's advice, happened upon a few Shoshones who took them to their chief, an impressive fellow by the name of Cameahwait. While translating for Lewis, Sacagawea suddenly recognized the chief as her now grown brother. Tears of happiness and laughter followed. Apparently pleased by this family reunion—and bribed by an army uniform, a pair of leggings, and a few handkerchiefs—this same chief provided the Corps of Discovery the many horses, together with an aging Indian guide named "Old Tobey," that were necessary for the next leg of their journey.

Since then, good fortune seems to abound here. The scenery of stark mountains and valleys is breathtaking; native cutthroat rise innocently and eagerly in the clear streams; and the dearth of people make solitude easy to find. No wonder I wanted to share this paradise with my wife.

But, like Lewis discovering the immense ranges to the west, this time happy anticipation has met with disappointment. The truck was but the latest calamity. It is only late June, and the weather is incredibly hot. Not even the most gullible trout could be caught in this high desert heat. Of course, the promise of air conditioning in this truck constituted a bad joke. To make matters worse, the only road through this valley was under serious repair. This necessitated interminable stops where the flag persons were as friendly as porcupines. No miraculous reunion here. We had little choice but to gaze onto many mountain peaks yet to climb.

By the third construction stop, I determined that Lewis and Clark's rate of progress equaled ours. They traveled this same mountain pass by horse, burdened by the incompetent Old Tobey. Exhibiting constant confidence, Old Tobey completely lost his way and crisscrossed the Continental Divide five times. The Corps of

THIS YOUR RIG?

Discovery was forced to cut though incredible underbrush and downed timber. These exertions were for no useful purpose—existing trails and passes could have easily transported the expedition north toward Lolo, the pass used by the Clearwater River Tribes to cross east into buffalo country. Sitting in the steamy truck, I comforted myself with the thought of William Clark struggling up what is so aptly named Lost Trail Pass only to see one of his horses stumble and plummet down a sheer cliff.

Trying to lift our spirits, I mentioned to Jess some cheerful banality, "At least we have plenty to eat." I then read from the guide book about the expedition's mounting hunger, the lack of game, and the need to kill their valuable horses for food. Jess did not respond, but she bravely smiled and looked out at the many mountain peaks.

Unlike the Corps of Discovery, I knew we were heading for a warm meal and a comfortable bed. Using atypical foresight, I had reserved the best room at Lochsa Lodge. Note the name, for it is the only place for food, gas, and lodging for 150 miles as one drops down Lolo Pass into the Idaho wilderness. I had a deep affection for this lodge. I first heard of it after camping out in the wilderness for two weeks straight. Upon learning of the possibility of a mattress under a roof, I immediately packed my gear and screamed into the night, down the twisting road for two hours until I reached this Nirvana: cold beer in jelly jars, a free pool table, and the softest sheets I had ever experienced. This place was bound to please Jessica, whose love of fishing, horses, hard ground, and camp food does not equal mine.

Cresting Lolo Pass yields one of the great sights in the continent. This is among the few spots where one can still see America precisely as Lewis and Clark did: endless firs and old-growth cedar carpeting the mountains as they wind westward. I chattered about the anticipated view to Jess and decided to lay it on thick. I added that the great historian Bernard DeVoto loved this site and often camped below while editing the Lewis and Clark journals. His final wish was to have his ashes spread over this pass. Upon cresting the pass, Jess and I searched the horizon. The tops of the nearest spruce were barely visible in the haze; the backdrop was a sickly, brownish-yellow impenetrable curtain of smoke. The air of nineteenth century London or twentieth century L.A. would have been clearer. The smoke poured into the truck as we struggled to wind up the reluctant windows. I had led us to the heart of the forest fires during this summer of intense heat and drought. The view was not some enthralling Bierstadt landscape; it was Dante's inferno.

We still proceeded onward. Like most fond memories, Lochsa Lodge should have been left in the past. The cabin, with its bare hanging light bulb, thin mattress, and ill-fitting polyester sheets, was dismal. Having reserved the only cabin with a private bath, I found a toilet with no seat behind a drapery. The beer, which I desperately needed as a mood adjuster, was still fine, but the food hit the bottom of the scale—truly hideous. Only the bulbous, slow flies that swarmed the dining room seemed to enjoy the kitchen's fare. As I lifted the paper napkin placed over my soggy chicken-fried steak in a vain attempt to protect it from the flies, I swore that Lewis, Clark, and their hungry men had dined better on horseflesh.

By late evening, I felt much more like the moody Lewis than the efficient and enthusiastic Clark. After all, it was precisely at this stage of the Corps of Discovery's journey—while camped along the banks of the Lochsa River—that Lewis wrote the most darkly introspective entry in his journal:

> *This day I completed my thirty first year, and*
> *conceived that I had in all human probability*

*now existed about half the period which I am to
remain in this Sublunary world. I reflected that I
had as yet done but little, very little, indeed, to
further the happiness of the human race or to
advance the information of the succeeding
generation. I viewed with regret the many hours I
have spent in indolence ....*

This from a man who was opening the American West, leading
an unparalleled territorial and scientific exploration, exhibiting
remarkable diplomatic skills with many Indian tribes, and
commanding the Corps of Discovery from coast to coast while
losing only one man. Historians use Lewis's birthday quote to
prove that he probably would have been diagnosed as bipolar in
today's psychological world. Still, as I lay on the thin mattress and
polyester sheets, I vainly tried not to think what this particular
forty-one-year-old had accomplished in comparison to the much
younger Lewis.

The next morning, like Lewis, "I dash from me the gloomy
thought." I set out on an itinerary of enjoyment and learning for my
wife. First on the schedule was the beautiful DeVoto Memorial
Cedar Grove, with its massive ancient trees and its inspiring
setting. Unfortunately, it was not to be. A frontiersman like Clark
would have been astonished to find an entire forest declared closed.
But some government bureaucrat decided to do just that in order to
expand the parking lot at the Memorial Grove. The bulldozers and
chain saws screamed, scraped and beeped while diminishing the
size of this incomparable stand of western cedars. No problem; the
next stop was to be an idyllic and romantic hot spring well off the
beaten path. Upon hiking in two rugged miles to reach it, we found
the spring crowded with Generation X types listening not to the
call of the western tanager but to Jimi Hendrix on a boom box and

sharing a bong. Gloomy thoughts began to reappear. Jess, noticing the thundercloud forming on my brow, urged a retreat rather than a frank confrontation in which I might warn the younger generation of the danger of "hours spent in indolence."

At this point, like the Corps of Discovery, I found the need for some local guidance. I may not have had the trusty Sacagawea, but there was a "recreational specialist" at the nearby U.S. Forest Service headquarters. This cheerful, uniformed federal employee, wearing a red nametag that confirmed that he was indeed a "recreational specialist," mapped out a gentle hike far from the three major wildfires still burning out of control. Thus, we set out along what Clark christened "Colt Killed Creek", a name reflecting that hunger once again struck the Corps and another horse was roasted. I remembered the creek—now renamed White Sands Creek in our kinder and gentler age—as a stunning example of Pacific Northwest forest hard against clear pools and riffles. And beautiful it remained. A mile down the path, however, the wind shifted and a cloud of stifling smoke descended. Even this tenderfoot realized that the fire had unexpectedly jumped a nearby ridge and was heading rapidly downhill toward these two wayfarers. As we labored up the trail at a jog, coughing and panting, I remembered that even the incompetent Old Tobey never walked anyone into a forest fire.

Back at the Lochsa Lodge bar, I decided that maybe those hours spent in indolence are not such a bad thing. At the free pool table, my luck wasn't changing. As a result, plenty of people wanted to play me for beers. And a colorful group it was—some had teeth, many displayed long knives strapped to their ample legs, a few had washed their hair at least once that summer, and camo was the fashion of choice. I could hardly refuse their requests to play. Despite certain cultural differences, we all had a jolly time with the satellite dish beaming in the Miss Universe pageant. Many of us liked Miss Ireland. I doubted if the enlisted men of the Corps of Discovery had this type of entertainment when they secretly made up some home brew just downstream from here.

My surveying of the talents of Miss Denmark ceased when another incredibly large man grasped my shoulder, pointed to Jess seated in a corner, and said, "That your gal? You best pay attention to that outfit."

There is something that turns one to chalk when you see the woman you love bravely sitting in a smoky bar with an untouched beer, watching Miss. Universe, deep in the Idaho wilderness. As tears welled up in her eyes, her only words were, "I just want to go home and spend my life with you."

On this trip we had not found some Northwest Passage of our own, probably because one does not exist. So, as did the Corps, we headed back East. Unlike Private John Colter, we would not stay and live in the Rocky Mountain West. Our voyage of discovery, however, was just beginning. We proceed onward.

Chapter Twelve: *The Sword from the Stone*

The massive oval table was made of highly polished bird's eye maple. I looked down at the beautiful wood momentarily as I prepared my answer. The entire setting was intentionally impressive. The huge conference room featured an entire glass wall providing a striking view of the historic Old State House, the leather chairs surrounding the table bore brass nameplates of past partners, a mahogany standing desk used by Daniel Webster sat ceremonially in the corner, an original Winslow Homer adorned one of the walls. Everything practically screamed that this was a law firm that catered to old Boston money.

At the opposite end of the table sat the firm's chairman. With a full head of thick white hair, a long, lined, patrician face, and fierce eyes, he was one of the old legal lions. A former president of the American Bar Association and an advisor to several presidents, he was not only a powerful presence, but also a powerful man. Two of his friends, dressed in the requisite blue, wool, pin-striped suits, flanked the chairman. The rest of the conference room occupants were less intimidating. Three female lawyers of different ages were dressed in dark business suits that featured severe jackets, skirts, and white blouses with either modest necklaces or frilly necklines. The remaining male lawyers sported either inexpensive suits or, in the case of the three criminal defense attorneys, sport coats with silk or linen shirts and no ties. I knew the defense attorneys and they clustered down at my end of the table as if saying that they had more in common with me than with the stern legal lion. Then there were a few "civilians" who were not lawyers but well-known community activists. These men and women wore casual clothes and kept looking around at the impressive setting. This collection was the Judicial Nominating Commission which, by long tradition, was to review the qualifications of each judicial nominee before the

Governor submitted the candidate to the Governor's Council for confirmation. Despite its name, the Judicial Nominating Commission did not nominate state court judges, the Governor did that; instead, its purpose, as created by some long-ago governor, was to assure the public that the Governor did nominate some unqualified political hack.

Having spent fifteen years as a federal prosecutor, I was ready for a change and dearly wanted to be a trial judge. Ever since clerking for a famous federal judge after law school, a judicial appointment had been my long-term dream. The current governor, who I had supervised at the U.S. Attorney's Office while she briefly worked there, had a soft spot for me. When she summoned me to her impressive office, she was her usual direct self, "Richard, I want to put you on the bench. This is your window of opportunity. I'm a black woman who ran on a criminal justice reform platform. Only I can appoint a hard-ass male WASP prosecutor and not take any heat." She gave her beautiful broad smile and added, "Now won't that shake up the old boys!"

Shake them up it did. As I vigorously indicted various white-collar frauds, including several old-line lawyers and law firms, I hardly thought of the consequences. These law firms and lawyers were amassing wealth by defrauding banks in a complex scheme and filing false federal forms to cover their tracks. Only the feds had the power and endurance to take them on. It was gratifying to take down the dishonest who were adept at using the levers of power and were not used to being questioned. Once the indictments were handed down and the arrests made, I saw their previous disdainful expressions change to confusion and astonishment. I never gave a thought to the long-term consequences. I was just doing my job. Perhaps I've always been a carpe diem kind of guy.

Little did I reckon that I would now be sitting in the conference room of one of the prestigious law firms under federal indictment, all thanks to my vigor. The current U.S. Attorney loved to recount the story of how the chairman of the now-indicted firm had approached him at some bar function and demanded my firing. But now the tables had turned, and the firm's chairman glared down the long length of the table as his friend peppered me with questions regarding my career. Finally, the chairman looked down at my resume, cleared his throat, and asked, "Mr. Wales, I see that you were a fly-fishing guide for several years, how did that past work experience prepare you for the rigors of the bench?"

I looked up from the bird's eye maple, stared forward, and responded, "It taught me patience." I paused and added, "It also taught me how to deal with different personalities. Both are rather valuable attributes for a judge."

One of the defense attorneys interrupted, "do you mean 'different' or 'difficult'?" He winked at me and tilted his head toward the chairman. The other two defense counsel laughed and a female lawyer turned toward me and smiled. I made the mistake of smiling back at her. The legal lion was not smiling, "Mr. Wales, do you think this proceeding is a joking matter? There is little worse than a judge who thinks he has a monopoly on wit and wisdom."

I looked toward the other end of the table and thought of what a pain in the ass this arrogant blow hard would be in a boat. "I do not think this is a joking matter at all. I take the fair enforcement of the law very seriously."

The table was silent, the three defense attorneys lowered their heads like fifth graders being reprimanded by the teacher. I felt my father's presence. I held back a grin as I thought of him striding to the other end of the table and taking a poke what he would have called "a *real* son of a bitch." The thought, however, was fleeting because the triumvirate at the opposite end of the table was now asking questions about a long-ago arrest in Montana. I quickly noted that it was a misunderstanding and emphasized that no criminal charges resulted. Then one of the striped blue suits questioned some enthusiastic closing I had made in a case. When I pointed out that the conviction had been affirmed on appeal and that the appeals court had found the closing proper, my answer was dismissed with a wave of the hand. "Mr. Wales," the lion replied as if patiently explaining matters to a slow school boy, "everyone knows you have won many cases. We also know that you *try* to portray yourself as some Robin Hood-like figure as you prosecute your so-called white-collar crime cases." He paused, looked around the table knowingly, and raised his voice slightly, "of course, we also know this is a façade since you are working for the all-powerful federal government." Again, he paused, raised his hands slightly from the table, and continued, "All of this, however, is beside the point because we are here to consider your judgment and temperament, not how many scalps you have taken."

Sometimes you have to sit quietly and take it.

One of the defense attorneys called the next day, "I'm sorry I broke up during the meeting. You got screwed. It was a close vote, but you lost. The fix was in from the start." I was not surprised. After all the hearing was held at a law firm which would soon plead guilty and dissolve after being in existence for one hundred and forty years. I was, however, severely disappointed. The phone rang again, it was one of the female lawyers, "I am so sorry. The proceeding was like a North Korean trial." As we commiserated, my secretary entered and told me that the Governor was on hold. She was not happy, "Those rich, white pricks! This isn't over. My legal counsel will be in contact." Without my having a chance to speak, she hung up.

When I broke the disappointing news to my wife Jess, she was incensed. She was fiercely protective of her relatively new husband, "No one is as qualified as you. There must be something we can do. Can we get them to reconsider?"

"No, the vote is final."

Jess let out a deep breath, shook her beautiful, long dark hair, and announced, "I am going to go down to that law firm and talk with that ass!" Being tall, in phenomenal shape, and with eyes flashing with anger, I had no doubt that she would be an intimidating presence. Like her Scottish ancestors roaming the Highlands and descending on some unwary Redcoats, she might bring considerable fear to those law firm Brahmins.

Jess was not gentle with her opinions. It was one of the many things that drew me to her. If I pushed, I knew there would be plenty of push back. I liked that—most of the time.

I tried to deflect her fury, "That sounds like something my father would do."

"I would have liked your father."

"Jess, he would have loved you. There simply is not much we can do. Let's go out to dinner and celebrate the loss."

Thanks to selective leaks from the Governor's office and others, the usually mundane decision of the Judicial Nominating Commission became front page news. The Governor, in the midst of a reelection bid, decided to make my rejection a campaign issue. She publicly vowed to ignore the advice of the Judicial Nominating Commission and pledged to nominate me for a high-level judgeship as soon as she was reelected. "I want judges," her press release read, "who will stand up and speak truth to power. What type of justice system allows powerful lawyers, from a firm allegedly involved in a criminal conspiracy, to prevent an extremely qualified prosecutor from being a judge? I want transparency and fairness, and I stand behind Richard Wales." Yikes, I thought, this type of attention was not what I had envisioned.

The Governor's Republican opponent joined the fray and pointed out that the present Governor had appointed the members of the Judicial Nominating Commission and that no governor had ever overruled the Commission's decisions. Both these points were correct, but the Boston papers liked the controversy and seemed to side with the Governor.

As the words flew and the campaign raged, I received a visit from the Governor's legal counsel. He said he wanted to relay a message from the Governor. We sat in my office as he explained that the campaign was reaching a critical stage. I nodded. Then he stated that the *Boston Globe* was pressing to interview me in order to run a profile. I nodded again, and he hurried to add, "That is *not* going to happen."

"Why not?" I asked.

The legal counsel shook his head. The Governor tells me you went to Yale Law School and that you fly fish. That's bad enough, but I have to ask you this question, "Do you really play squash?'

I sensed where this meeting was heading, "I went to Yale on a full scholarship, and I am not a very good squash player."

"Yeah, but none of this plays into our David versus Goliath narrative. Look, we have great respect for you, but the Governor said, and I quote, 'Tell Wales that he looks better from afar than up close. He should get out of town without delay.'"

I laughed and thought of her direct manner and husky voice, "Tell the Governor that I am going home immediately and will try to convince my wife that we should flee the Commonwealth."

I knew this would not be easy to accomplish. Jess was a remarkable public-school teacher and loved her second-grade class. She would never agree to abandon the students in the middle of the semester. And, although I had not been married long, I suspected that my sudden absence would not help the romance, a romance that had been challenged during our recent trip to Lolo Pass.

When I told Jess of the latest development, the response was quick and firm, "What! I can't leave my class. Who is the Governor to order you to go into hiding? Maybe I should talk to her, woman to woman, and set her straight." Jess paused and lowered her voice, "She should let you talk to the press instead of requiring you to wimp out with your 'no comment' responses. She's probably afraid you will take the spotlight away from her."

For a moment I basked in the unconditional support of the newly married and, then, returned to reality. I explained that the Governor had gone out on a limb for me and that I felt bound to honor her request. Jess breathed deeply, smiled, and agreed that it would be nice to avoid all the press attention every time we went out in public. "After all," she reasoned, "you always look irritated in those photos the newspapers print."

After a quiet dinner during which we both avoided the topic, Jess stated with her usual certainty, "I will miss you terribly, but you should get away for a while and return around election day. It's only ten days away."

For once I argued against taking a vacation. I truly did not want to leave Jess. I smiled every time she entered a room. Then she mentioned her discovery of that morning. Several students in her class were infected with head lice. Jess mentioned it casually and airily informed me that head lice are an expected event in almost every school. She laughed at my horrified reaction. "It's not that big a deal. Lice are just small insects that are killed with a special shampoo. It's not like I have them—yet." She laughed again.

I had endured Jess returning home with assorted, and apparently endless, germs from her classroom—most of which she seemed immune to after many years of teaching, but all of which had laid me low. Head lice, however, held a place of special horror. I booked a flight to Miami, rented a car, and headed south to Big Pine Key.

My friend Jack was fishing around Big Pine Key. I didn't know precisely where, but it is not that big an island. Even if I could not find him, he was such a character that a few inquiries would produce results. Sure enough, a very young waitress at a local dockside bar giggled when I described Jack and correctly predicted that "Mr. Jack" would arrive for a drink at eight that evening. She continued, "But don't interrupt us now, we're going on a date later tonight." I tried to gauge her age. She looked like a developing fourteen-year-old.

"No problem. I just wanted to locate 'Mr. Jack' and I obviously have."

I pitched my small tent next to Jack's sleeping bag hidden in the brush of some public picnic area bordering U.S. Route 1. The first night I was startled by the large land crabs that scuttled through the leaf litter and attempted to enter bag. Jack quickly advised that I should not turn on a flashlight because it might alert police to our presence and result in eviction from what Jack considered a pristine camping site. He added, "The crabs mostly climb over you. They usually don't try to get into your sleeping bag." I was glad Jess was far away in the civilized Commonwealth.

The entire trip was like being homeless while fishing with expensive fly gear. We would hunt bonefish near the drone of Route 1 or trespass into seaside subdivisions and poach the flats when the tide began to rise. Jack's vision was remarkable and he would point out the bonefish, heads down and tails bobbing, as they silently coasted in with the tide. The best time was the evenings as the light faded and the sky turned pink and purple. This, however, was also when the large lemon sharks would also swim up onto the flats. Even I could see the shark fins and their impressive wakes. When the sharks became numerous, or when one bumped my leg, we quickly left for the dockside bar.

Jack was the perfect companion for he never followed any political event and had no interest in my sudden notoriety. Jack was all fishing, most of the time. Nor was Jack even slightly interested in most legal matters. Over a dockside beer, he only asked one legal question, "Is it really true that having sex with a sixteen-year-old is a criminal offense?" When I told him that statutory rape consisted of having sex with anyone under the age of sixteen, Jack looked down and silently pondered this information. As the silence continued, it slowly dawned on me that the Governor did not have this type of vacation or this type of companion in mind when she suggested that I leave town. On the other hand, in my brushy—albeit illegal—campsite, I was well hidden from any *Boston Globe* reporter.

One day the tide began to rise at midday. The wind was pleasantly light and merely ruffled the surface of the incoming sea. Jack, claiming that only small fish would be feeding in the bright sun, did not wade out onto the large flat. Instead he lay down in the shade of an Australian pine and closed his eyes.

I scanned the water and slowly moved across the very shallow bay. As Jack predicted, I saw nothing until suddenly the distinctive, sickle shaped tail of a permit flashed in the sun. I had never seen a permit outside of sporting magazines and was no expert. I knew, however, that catching a permit on a fly was the equivalent of pulling the sword from the stone. Permit are big, strong fish that feed occasionally on bonefish flats. They are notoriously spooky in the rare instances that they enter shallow water. Many long-time salt water anglers never get a shot at a permit, never mind hook one. Here, however, was my very own permit, obviously tipping its large head down to the sandy bottom, feeding, and slowly heading toward me. I had read that permit often feed on crabs, and, several years ago, I had purchased a couple of intricate flies that imitated small crabs. The problem with a crab fly is that it is bulky and heavy. Not a problem for an expert caster, but a real challenge for me. So off came the small, shrimp-like bonefish fly and on went the crab imitation. I stood still, watched the permit continue toward me, stripped the fly line off my reel, held the loose line in my left hand, and timed my cast.

Usually the best way to measure the distance of a cast and get the heavy fly line moving toward the target is to cast the line but not let it touch the surface, a so-called false cast, and, then, sweep the line back behind you once more and cast to the target and let your fly land softly in front of the fish. I sensed that a false cast would spook this most wary of fish so I was left with a more difficult cast involving a short, swift backcast and then shooting the line forward. I shook some line out from the tip of the rod for the backcast, yanked the rod back quickly, and then gave the line a sharp pull, let go, and shot the heavy fly forward. I was rather proud of myself as I watched the fly line straighten like an arrow toward the permit. As I said, this is not an easy cast. The crab fly, however, did not settle gently in front of the hungry permit, instead it was propelled like a heat-seeking missile onto the permit's exposed back, skipped like a stone, and clunked off its lifted tail. The permit exploded and fled with lightning speed. The flat suddenly seemed very empty, and I trudged back to the sleeping Jack.

I described my failure to Jack, a man who had never held a full-time job after an Air Force stint in Viet Nam and literally fished most every day. He shrugged and said, "You're lucky. I've never even seen a permit."

On my last day in exile, we walked through a few small neighborhoods seeking access to the canals that bordered many of the homes. Our quarry was the baby tarpon that cruised through the canals and attacked any bright streamer. Once hooked, these handsome silver fish, ranging up to three feet in length, would jump repeatedly and crash back to the water. I was playing a beautiful tarpon from a seemingly abandoned dock when I heard the distinctive sound of a gun being racked. I turned and saw a semi-automatic pistol being pointed at me by an overweight, unshaven man wearing a L.A. Lakers uniform—not just the jersey, but also the gold shorts with the purple side stripes and impressive, high-top sneakers.

He uttered various threats. I sputtered many apologies and took off. When I ran into Jack emerging from another cul-de-sac, I breathlessly related my encounter. Jack smiled, "Yeah, he's not a member of the basketball team. He's just a drug dealer that everyone stays away from. I should have told you to avoid that street."

As I headed toward Miami and my flight home, I thought of my return to the rough and tumble of Massachusetts politics. It all seemed rather placid compared to the lemon sharks, land crabs, and drug dealers.

When I arrived at Logan Airport, Jess ran toward me, jumped, and hugged me. I stumbled, and we collapsed on the baggage claim floor laughing and kissing. The pieces of the puzzle shifted, fit together perfectly, and grounded my world. Jess lay on top of me, staring into my face, smiling. I told her that she should have married a stronger man, and we kissed more. When we rose, people smiled at us and a few clapped as if celebrating the intensity of early love.

On the ride home, Jess mentioned that the classroom head lice had been eradicated. I tried to hide my elation.

The next day we voted and watched the results of a close election. By midnight, the Republican opponent conceded and the Governor reveled in her reelection. Two days later, Jess and I were escorted into the Governor's State House chambers. After the Governor quickly hugged me, she turned to Jess, smiled, held her hand and said, "I truly have been looking forward to meeting the woman who married this long-time bachelor."

Jess glanced over at me, and then turned her blue-green eyes toward the Governor, "Oh he's sometimes a handful. That aside, Governor, you have made a good choice."

The governor chuckled, "I am certain I have." She then signaled for the press to join us for an announcement. As the reporters filed in, she leaned toward me and whispered, "Let me do the talking."

The governor nominated me to the highest state trial court, and she used her considerable political muscle to assure a quick confirmation.

THE SWORD FROM THE STONE

As I was sworn in as a judge, I understood that this was one of those precious moments in life when everything had broken my way. Like making a perfect cast that lands softly in front of a hungry permit.

Chapter Thirteen: *Bedtime Stories*

The evening ritual varies but little. First a game of dinosaurs. I am usually one of the meat eaters—an Allosaurus, Dilophosaurus, or even the fearsome T-Rex. It all depends on the particular period—Triassic, Jurassic or Cretaceous—for the seven-year-old is an expert on such matters. He prefers to be a gentle plant eater, although often one with horns or a clubbed tail, so that his father will chase him but he will have defenses in the ensuring wrestle. The five-year old often chooses to be a small, fast sort—say a Coelophysis—who can run about and irritate with impunity.

This drama lasts for ten or fifteen minutes until their aged father admits exhaustion and hauls them to the bathtub. Incredibly realistic humpback, blue, or gray whales accompany them—or even a genuinely sinking Titanic—and I sit on the floor besides them. The conversation mostly drifts to make-believe games and similar banter between the two boys.

These bath scenes bring me back to my childhood. Being the only boy sandwiched between four sisters, I never enjoyed a communal tub with a brother. Indeed, with four sisters it was hard to get into the tub at all. My sisters loved to soak in the tub while reading books that seemed to me impossibly long and boring. Still stacked on the shelves of my sisters' shared home are well-watered editions of *Gone with the Wind*, *Little Women*, and a seemingly full collection of Agatha Christie mysteries—with their expanded bindings and buckled pages. Occasionally, when the bathtub was available, I would shed my clothes and sink slowly into that pink porcelain tub, only to have my older sister burst from the bath closet to laugh at my exposed genitalia.

Before such sisterly assaults, when I was younger, my father would sit next to me as I stared at the gaps in the bathroom tiling, expecting to see yet another terrifying centipede crawl out. He would calm my nerves, and then I would avoid any of his questions by beginning an interrogation of my own. One line of questioning I often pursued was my father's World War II experience amphibiously assaulting various South Pacific islands. Like many young boys, blood, gore and guts were fascinating—especially the blood and guts of those stiff Nazis or tricky Japs. Although I later learned from other sources that my father's Army unit suffered massive casualties in hand-to-hand combat and that, after most of the officers had been killed, he received field promotions from private to first lieutenant, my father proved completely resistant to my inquiries. He would tell me of Filipino customs and the interesting jungle islands to the north. I was not interested in a *National Geographic* lesson, so I pressed on. Then I would hear of beach landings, poor food, half-track armored vehicles, and once even a Kamikaze attack on a ship. But he would end the conversation before I could get to the blood and gore.

One time, exasperated, I directly asked, "But Dad, did you ever kill anybody?" The response from this college professor was a simple "Yes, Rich, I killed many men, but I do not like to talk about it." It was said in that indefinable parental tone that left no doubt that the discussion was over then and for always. It was a tone my father had no trouble finding, but the same cannot be said for his son. I have tried to mimic the same speech pattern with my sons, but it never works. Fortunately, I can always fall back upon hair washing, which always produces a rapid change of subject.

After the bath, my two boys are ready for the highlight of the evening: bedtime stories. Each boy selects one book or story, and their father has the right to supplement with a third reading. I am always somewhat surprised by public reminders to parents of the importance of reading to their children—as though it was a novel or forgotten practice. At least in my family, it always has been a ritual.

One of my earliest memories is my mother reading to me a story about the Sandman who comes each night to put us to sleep by sprinkling magic sand over our eyes. Taken by the story, I insisted that I wanted to see the Sandman come. My mother, who, while completely loving, was hardly over-protective in her child rearing, agreed that I could wait for him. She took my small rush-bottomed chair out to the top of a small rise beside the farm house we rented. And there in the deep twilight in rural southern Virginia I sat alone—age three or four—wrapped in a blanket. Sure enough, I was told as I woke in my bed the next morning that the Sandman had come, put me to sleep in my chair, and then carried me into bed.

Several years later, my mother was reading to her ever-increasing brood of children a story from one of Thornton Burgess's collections—a staple in our household. Perhaps it was one of Jimmy Skunk's or Johnny Chuck's adventures. It was the evening after a hectic day. My mother's father had died suddenly, and the house had been in a chaotic state ever since the phone call. I remember little about the day except the evening storytelling. We were all perched on my older sister's bed; my mother was reading with her usual animation about the animals in the green meadows with old Mother West Wind and the Merry Breezes. Suddenly we heard the soft mournful call of a whippoorwill—a sound that was rare even then. Perhaps it was the bird's call, or the exhaustion of the day, but my mother lowered her head and began to weep. My sisters and I were stunned as my father gently led her away and finished that and then another story. The second story was a spirited rendition of the crafty Reddy Fox, who was forever trying to catch Peter Rabbit and while often being chased by Bowser the

Hound. It was such a good tale that I went to sleep without a thought of my mother's tears. But whenever I hear a whippoorwill at dusk, I am always that boy sitting on the bed watching his mother.

My boys select two fine stories for the evening: *Owl Moon* by Jane Yodel and a *Frog and Toad* tale by Elliot Lobel. They sit on the bed, each on one side of their father. By the second story, I feel their heads softly rest on my arms. My selection this evening is an illustrated version of the Robert Frost poem, "Birches." I begin by attempting to explain what a poem is. Not an easy task, especially after a long day in court and a spirited session as a T Rex. I am interrupted by my older son who, in typical fashion, asks a question that is not directly on point but is important: "Daddy, why do you always read to us?"

For once I have an easy, honest, and prompt response. "Because, Rich, I know of no better way to show my love for my two boys." My response is quick for I have been thinking of an incident when I was about six years older than Rich: that impossible time of early adolescence when hormones are rapidly rising and you have just reached the unquestionable conclusion that you know everything and are certain of even more. The family is seated around the dinner table and my older sister is behaving poorly. She is insisting on going out on a date with some undesirable older fellow who rides a motorcycle. My father, whose patience approached Job's but whose temper—when finally provoked was like a thunder bolt from Thor—had informed her that such a date could not take place on a weekday, perhaps on a weekend. My sister threw down her fork, rattling the plate, and stormed away from the table. My father rose and I, for some unfathomable reason, jumped up to defend my sister's rotten judgment and poor manners. "Don't you bother her," I screamed in his face. And then perhaps impressed with my rapidly developing body or, more likely, in the grip of Freudian adolescent insanity, I shoved him harshly and cocked my fist. My father quickly batted away my fist and gave a soft but sure opened handed slap to my cheek. Feigning physical pain—but in truth feeling ashamed and humiliated—I rushed to my room in tears.

A half-hour later, my father entered and sat on my bedside. He did not apologize. Of course, he had done nothing for which to apologize. And he was wise enough not to ask for an apology from a thirteen-year-old boy. Instead, he picked up the book on the bedside table. The title was *The Pond*, a wonderful book by Robert Murphy about a young boy growing up in the rural south. My father had given it to me that Christmas, while he was on a teaching sabbatical and we were living in the old mill at the juncture of the Artichoke and Merrimack rivers. He always inscribed every book he gave, and this inscription read: "A book about a boy who had only one pond, for a boy who has two rivers." Opening the book to the bookmark, he began to read to me. He had not read me a story for several years, but he did not hesitate as he read an entire chapter. And then, without a word, he kissed me on the same cheek, and left.

I begin reading the Robert Frost poem. Almost immediately, I realize it is too advanced for the boys and that it speaks more to me than to them. But the boys lean more heavily against me and I read on:

> *Some boy too far from town to learn baseball,*
> *whose only play was what he found himself. . . .*
> *So was I once myself a swinger of birches and so*
> *I dream of going back to be.*

I finish the poem, surprised that the boys sat through it quietly. I look down at my younger son, Robert, and see that he is not asleep.

Instead, his eyes are wide open and he asks: "Daddy, I love birch trees, can we swing on one sometime together?" "Yeah," adds his older brother, "and don't swing so much you go straight up into the sky or fall boom and crash into the ground."

They race off to their bunk beds. I kiss them good night and turn off the light.

As I reshelf the books, my thoughts jump from Johnny Chuck, to the sand man, and my parents, the whippoorwill call, and that boy climbing up the birch trees. I wonder how I will handle a thirteen-year-old boy, never mind two. It is easier to be a swinger of birches than a father. But, often, the stories help.

154

Chapter Fourteen: *Striped Blast*

Fly fishing with children is overrated. Any magazine or catalog picture that shows the grinning young lad and slightly graying dad casting or catching together in happy union is a fraud. If you have actually embarked on these multi-generational fishing trips, you know how quickly complaints burst forth concerning bugs, cold, and boredom. Such a communion of young and old anglers is hardly conducive to Thoreau-like bonding with nature or hard-driving, rip-the-lips fishing. This reality is based on a simple truth: fishing, particularly fly fishing, is a selfish pursuit.

Luckily all rules have their exceptions. There are those sweet lapses when the light slants in a certain way to illuminate all the beauty, the wind ceases and the glassy currents reveal thousands of swirls, the mosquitoes disappear, and the striped bass are dumb and hungry.

My older son is only eleven, but he is a much different child than his father at that age. He has strengths of courage, patience, determination, and caring that never crossed my young mind or creased my adolescent soul. While challenged in many ways, he can read through most any bookshelf. His idea of a good time is not to traipse the fields and swing on birches. He will never know the joy of football, basketball, or any team sport. Nirvana to him is a solitary trip to the library. While his father at eleven years old would daydream over the purple prose of *Field & Stream* magazine, he studies books on the Middle Ages, the Great Depression, and global warming. But what good is a father if he does not at least try to bend his son to the father's passions?

So it is that I labor to plant the seed in his mind for yet another attempt at a father-and-son fishing trip. Late spring finally has arrived. The tin boat is in, and miraculously I have even remembered to tune up the outboard motor. The tide will crest early morning, and then the striped bass will be abundant on the falling tide. "But Dad, I lost my hat the last time we went out on the boat." Another ball cap identical to the first has been purchased, and he can use either his beginner fly rod or a spin cast rod. I will pack both together with a favorite snack. "Dad, would it be O.K. if I didn't go? 5 A.M. is early and the mosquitoes will be out." I detail the wonders of DEET and shamelessly give a soulful look.

Sure enough, 5 A.M. is early and clouds of mosquitoes hug the shore. But, as I said, my son is caring and patient and he never wants to disappoint his difficult father. With both hands clutching his cap, we cast off and are away. Sweeping along with the massive current of a river as big as the Merrimack makes me feel as free as Huck Finn. The light breeze scarcely ripples the surface. The early gray light silhouettes the massive pines and oaks along the bank, and the pink horizon augurs a fair day. With this first light, the world is full of promise.

We skim along the surface. Our destination is a series of islands in the middle of the river where the Atlantic salt mixes thoroughly with the snow melt from New Hampshire. I know that downstream Joppa Flat will be full of boats and anglers but here we will be surprisingly alone. We drift past the islands with their granite outcroppings. The tide has just turned, and the small marsh creeks are spilling out into the river channels. Not a bug bothers us, but the river surface is empty. I tell my son to wait. I make the foolish promise that in just a minute he will see fish. Of course, I am setting him up for disappointment. It may be just another boring venture of few fish, many a tangle, and increasingly stressful parental commands.

STRIPED BLAST

I am looking at my beautiful boy when I see that, for once, the magic is with me. His entire face lights up and his eyes dance. And for good reason. I turn and see that the calm surface has erupted into a series of swirls. The bass are so close to the surface that fins and tails are in the air. The river is alive for as far as one can see. And then the words any father loves to hear, "You're right, Dad!"

It is a marvel. Most of these fish have traveled from the Chesapeake, along hundreds of coastal miles, past the seals, up the river, to now feast upon these New England herring. I have seen this abundance before but, with my excited son at my side, I now see it with fresh eyes. As we drift with the fish, I can actually hear the swirls. The slapping tails and jumping herring are within arm's reach. I can feel the small tin boat shake as my son hums and involuntarily hops from one foot to another in joy. As the light comes up everything seems so pure, so young and innocent. I look at the natural beauty reflected in my son's lovely face and, instead of reaching for my eight-weight rod, I stop and—to my surprise— whisper. I whisper that I hope this feeling will never end, that my son will always be so filled with joy, that he will always be excited by nature and the dawning of a new day.

I am in no hurry, but my son is. His fly rod is rigged with just the right fly but he cannot take his eyes off the fish. He fumbles for his rod and drops it twice. I ask him if he wants me to cast and he can retrieve the bulky Deceiver. And that is what we do. The fishing is downright easy. The fish hurl themselves at the blue-and-white fly and run with the current. My son reels and strains and insists on touching the side of each striped fish before watching it swim away. Always he asks, "The fish will be O.K., right?" I reassure, strip out line, cast again, and hand the rod to him. It is a wonderful partnership.

The magic cannot last. Luckily it lingers for a long time, though, and only slowly fades away with the fish. Yet we are still in its sway. We motor back against the rushing tide. My son turns, both hands still clutching the ball cap, and with a big smile and announces, "Dad, that was a striped blast. Get it?" Even then I know I have not converted him into an avid fishing companion. He will not be helping his aged father negotiate the rocks along the stream or use his better eyesight to identify the hatch. He is with me out of love for me, not the sport. He continues to smile as I look at his perfect face. I smile back, raise my hat to the rising sun, give a full-throated "Yeeehaah," and push the throttle.

Chapter Fifteen: *Swimming the Grey's*

My younger son can fill the empty spaces of the West and of the mind.

"Hey, Daddy, can I have another piece of chicken with the sauce on it?"

"Yes, it's called barbecued chicken. Just make sure to use a napkin."

My eight-year-old son and I are rolling through a Wyoming national forest filled with green spruce against an impossibly blue sky. The back seat of the rented Ford Explorer already shows signs of many a meal. I am sure that the seat cushion is the only napkin known to my son.

"This is great, Daddy. I am so happy, just you and me."

"I'm happy, too. Don't you miss Mom and Rich?"

"Well, a little, but they don't like camping and fishing as much as I do. Remember that big whitefish I caught last year? You know, Daddy, those whitefish are really hard to catch. Much harder than trout. They have those little mouths. I hope I catch one this year." It would break his heart to know that most fisherman scorn the lowly whitefish with its sucker-like mouth and bland coloring.

My son Robert is the prototypical second child with plenty of confidence and a big personality. I wonder if our destination, the Grey's River, has many of those sporting whitefish.

This car trip is typical of our last week together. The questions are non-stop. At age eight, my son has not yet even thought of venturing to the silent, sullen, dark-side-of-the-moon adolescence where iPods and video games replace conversation.

"Hey, Daddy, what are those birds with the long necks? Not the herons, but the others?"

My response: "Sandhill cranes."

"Why do they call them cranes? I thought you saw those with bulldozers. Do you get it Daddy? It's a joke."

"Why don't we have those cranes in Massachusetts?"

"How come they have dirt roads out here?"

"Can I roll down the window? I don't feel too good. My stomach hurts."

"Hey, Daddy, you know, it feels much better when you throw up. Especially if you have orange soda afterwards. Do we have any more orange soda?"

Then, as he is prone to do, he pauses for about ten seconds, which must seem an eternity to him, and announces, with great sincerity and enthusiasm, "I love you so much."

I assure him that I also love him. In fact, his presence taught me a truth about love. Convincing a forty-five-year old who is entranced with his first born to agree to a second child takes a bit of encouragement and, then, some tough thought. Like many an inexperienced parent, I thought that I could not possibly love another child as much as my first. But then the revelation comes. It descends like a summer thunderclap when you hold that small, crying, squirming body as he opens his blue eyes for the first time. Love is not some finite matter stored in a well and doled out in measures. Love is complete and infinite. This is a truth—for most. Yet experience gleaned from negotiating the world and sitting on the bench has taught me the sad fact that the infinity of love is not felt by all.

SWIMMING THE GREY'S

As I swerve to avoid a pothole, I realize that my son's running commentary has prevented such introspective thoughts on this trip. That may be a good thing or else I begin sounding like some New Age self-help book. As if on cue, he pipes up: "Aren't I being a good sport? I haven't even asked how much longer. Are you proud of me?"

I am proud of him. We drive twenty miles up the dirt road bordering the beautiful Grey's River, and he complains only briefly about the many miles. The water looks ideal: riffles, pools, and runs bordered by willow banks and gravel bars.

The Grey's River is something special in Wyoming. Wyoming is a state that guards the right of private property more jealously than any other. Remember, this is the land of Dick Cheney and his cohorts. It is the reddest of the red states. Not only is there no stream-access law—unlike its more generous neighbors of Montana and Idaho—a landowner owns even the bottom of the river on his or her property. If you anchor in the middle of most any Wyoming river, you are trespassing. Fortunately, the Grey's runs entirely through a national forest until it meets up with the Snake. Thus, it is blessedly public in this land of the protected and the selfish.

We finally pull over at a promising camp site. Robert walks around and declares it perfect. He cannot wait to help lug out the tent, sleeping bags, cooler, and assorted gear that astounds and fascinates him.

"How does the lantern work? Do you use batteries? Can I light it now? When it gets dark, will it be scary? Can I just light one match now?"

The erection of the tent seems to him almost a marvel. "Can I get in it now? Which side do you want? Are you going to snore tonight? When do we go fishing?"

We break out the fishing tackle. I carefully put together my custom-made, four-weight rod while Robert practices casting his Zebco. " I like the spinners, but can I use the Jitterbug first? Or maybe this one with the propeller on the back? What's this supposed to look like to the fish? Do fish really eat frogs? How about hot dogs? Why don't we have a lure that looks like a hot dog? I think I'll invent the hot dog lure. It will be Robert's Hot Dog, and it will catch lots of big whitefish."

The shallow riffles, rocky runs, and crystal pools of the Grey's are not exactly the slow bass-filled, lily-pad-choked waters for which the chunky Jitterbug was designed. So I am not surprised when the Zebco rod-reel-combo is put aside. But this does not mean that the fishing is over.

With Robert fishing is a full contact sport. Often, he becomes one with his environment. Instead of waders and a vest, Robert's fishing outfit is a swim suit and a pair of swim goggles. When the fish do not rise to his lure, Robert joins the fish. No matter how icy the stream, he loves swimming through the pools, spying the trout (or better yet whitefish) and pursuing them like an extremely oversized otter. It is not unusual to see him kicking furiously around a pool in circles and then surfacing with the announcement that he has just touched a big one.

This conduct would be frowned upon on the River Test, and it ain't too appreciated even in the high, wide, and lonesome West. Other anglers give us a very wide berth. I am wise enough to fish well upstream of Robert's touch-and-release activities. Still, I tempt nothing to rise. Hoppers, PMDs, and Royal Wulffs drift undisturbed. My efforts are not helped by a voice just down around the bend, "Daddy, there are some big ones here, I'll send them up to you." Sure enough, a few chunky but terrified cutthroat are soon steaming through the riffles and into my pool. They undoubtedly communicate to any living matter below the surface that all should hide from the Armageddon downstream.

"How come you haven't caught anything? Daddy, I'm getting hungry. Can we go back to camp soon?"

A problem with Robert's fishing outfit is revealed when we come in contact with the willows and sage that line the banks. Wails of pain come as he tries to walk through the streamside vegetation. Even at the tender age of eight, a middle linebacker-type body is not easy to lift for any length of time. At least not for this increasingly weak and feeble soul. After much straining, a little swearing, and a couple of trips to collect the fishing gear, we make it back to the car.

"I'm going to tell Mumma that you said god damn. You told me not to say that. Remember?"

I build and start the fire, and it has its usual hypnotic effect. With a single malt at hand, the Grey's River gurgling in the background, the sandhill cranes calling with their distinctive rattle, the last sunlight of the day slanting into this beautiful valley, all is well. I remind myself that I am a very lucky man.

"Hey, Daddy, did you bring the marshmallows? Did you remember the chocolate bars?"

"Good. I love you, Daddy."

My son's words deepen my feeling of peace, satisfaction and love. It is a moment of grace which is rare in this chaotic world. Rare and, almost always, fleeting.

Suddenly the roar of a pack of ATVs breaks the peace of the valley. Eight of these big wheeled creatures spring from the nearby cottonwoods where a large group of decidedly red-neck sorts have set up a substantial encampment that I did not anticipate. The perils of public land. They swerve toward us with headlights blazing. Most of the drivers wave, and one yells over the din, "Hi neighbor!"

"Hey, Daddy those are neat. Look at all of them. Awesome, look at all the dust. The dust is coming right over here. Can I buy one of those soon? That would be so cool. I could ride around, go swimming, ride some more, crash into things. You and me. Just like the video games at the arcade. Can we get two sometime?"

I lift my eyes up to the rocky outcropping and notice that it has faded from a warm ochre to a dull gray. The sun has set. Dick Cheney is somewhere on a private preserve well away from my ATV neighbors. He may be savoring the call of an owl or the yip of a coyote in his pristine wilderness enclave while I listen to the din of four-wheelers and smell gas exhaust. No one but he is fishing his sacred stream. Maybe my Scotch has faded visions of Cheney's snarling expression and his alarming political views for I check myself and try to be more charitable. Maybe, putting aside dramatic differences in politics and wealth, we may not be that different. He has two daughters and probably has experienced the infinite nature of love. Still, I smugly think, he will never know the joy of an eight-year-old human otter. I smile at the thought.

Chapter Sixteen: *Don't You Want to Be an Outlaw?*

The National Park Service can put my teeth on edge. Irritation bubbles within whenever those rangers tell me where to camp, cook, or crap in the wilderness. Don't get me wrong. In general, the NPS is wonderful. It saves land from development and allows we modest-income taxpayers to enjoy vistas from sea to shining sea. I can almost hear Woody singing about this land is your land.... I suppose it's the same old story: government regulation is fine, except when it applies to you.

I don't mind rules or laws or regulations. Hell, I'm a judge, and I apply the law most every day. I pay my taxes and file the required ethics forms. Indeed, I have a reputation for being rather strict with lawbreakers.

Take this example: a convicted defendant awaiting sentencing decided to exercise his "right of allocution" at a recent hearing. This means that the convict, undoubtedly against the advice of counsel, wanted to address me after the jury found him guilty and before I handed down the sentence. He began by asking me a question, "Judge, you know what they call this courthouse?" He didn't wait for my answer. "The smokehouse, that's what they call it, because we come before you, get our trial, and then we get smoked. You're fair, I guess; but, then, you smoke us after trial." By this point, his lawyer was practically pulling the defendant down into a chair and telling him to shut up.

I have no memory of what sentence Mr. Smokehouse received, but any adequate judge will tell you that determining what punishment to hand out is the most difficult and draining part of the job—only slightly more difficult than avoiding a comatose state while presiding over a seven-week patent or copyright trial. It all wears you down. Every time the cuffs snap on and the felon is shuffled out of the courtroom family members cry, you feel bad— but, truth be told, the convict feels a lot worse. Let's face it. I'm one of the guys who imposes law and order on the underclass of thieves, drug dealers, con men, the deranged or stupid, the shooters and rapists. That is what state court judges do.

I wanted to temporarily escape from law and order. That was my aim as I hiked into the quietest corner of Yellowstone. Be careful what you wish for.

Being married to a beautiful and caring woman, who would rather eat nails than camp in the Yellowstone backcountry, I was sent off alone. Jess would care for our two sons. Armed with this hall pass, I didn't delay.

I chose the remote southwest corner of Yellowstone because it offered beauty, uncrowded fishing, and a chance at redemption. Years earlier I had attempted to camp along the Falls River in this part of the Park, but a charging male grizzly ran me out. This time, I told myself, I would succeed. Also, I would carry bear spray.

The Bechler Ranger Station was a necessary burden. One must pay Uncle Sam and fill out the necessary paper work before being assigned a numbered campsite and heading into the Yellowstone backcountry. Just two minutes in the ranger's station reinforced that a lot had changed since John Colter came traipsing through this area. Although parts of Yellowstone are still plenty wild, it is girded and guarded by government bureaucracy. Fortunately, in this instance, governmental bureaucracy came in an attractive package. A young, fit, slightly plump female ranger wearing a snug gray shirt and tight green pants took my money and issued a backcountry camping permit. Handing the permit to me, she emphasized that it must be posted on my tent as soon as I arrived at the campsite. I looked into her clear, brown eyes and agreed. Alone in the quiet old building, she must have been bored or lonely because she continued the conversation. I asked her name, where she was from, how did she like being a park ranger. The answers were: Cassandra Cougar, from back East, and loved the job except for the horses. I had six miles to hike, so I bid goodbye, noticing that her chestnut-brown hair had golden streaks near her temples.

Three remarkably fit Aussies were hoisting small day packs when I arrived at the trailhead. As if from some Hollywood backlot, all were friendly and ruggedly handsome. It was their first time in the Yellowstone backcountry, and they were excited to begin their "through hike" to Old Faithful. A "through hike" in this area consists of an approximately thirty-five-mile wilderness hike through the Bechler River meadows which concludes once one stumbles upon the tour busses crowding the Old Faithful geyser. One must overcome bogs, mosquitoes, moose, and bears and find a very faint trial that skirts the river. This is usually a three-night journey; my new Aussie friends planned to hike it in a day and celebrate merrily at the bar at Old Faithful Inn that evening. The next day they would hike right back to this trailhead. I thought of my designated campsite six level miles ahead and felt like a slug.

As they set out, one turned to me with a smile: "Join us, mate?" I quickly declined and they charged up the trail.

The day was glorious, with sun spilling through the lodgepole pines and a slight breeze stirring. I stopped to listen to the liquid call of a Swainson's thrush once I found the sign post for my campsite. No bears, no humans, nothing, just beauty and a feeling of peace mixed with some sweat. The campsite was secluded, about a half mile off the trail and close to the small, sparkling Mountain Ash Creek. Tent erected, I decided to rebel against the Man and not attach my camping permit to the top pole. Feeling at one with the tax-refusing Henry David Thoreau, I went in search of kindling.

As I retraced my steps, I collected fallen twigs and broken mossy branches and then heard a distinctly feminine "Oh shit!" Dropping my load, I jogged toward the trail, and there was the uniformed Ms. Cougar sitting on her rump beside a large chestnut quarter horse. The horse was remarkably patient, looking back at its former rider while the saddle hung crookedly on its back. Affecting a Gary Cooper saunter, I picked up the loose reins and inquired if she was all right.

"I'm fine. I don't know what happened." She brushed off her pants and reddened a bit.

Feeling like an old hand, I tried to slow my speech to a Western pace. "The cinch probably loosened. Let me fix this. We'll walk the horse for a bit and tighten it again." Man, I thought, my life-long friend Mark, who had become an expert horseman while I remained a complete dude, would laugh if he saw this scene and heard my pathetic banter.

She confessed, "I hate these damn horses. What kind of backcountry ranger doesn't know how to ride? Beyond a walk, I'm hopeless. I have to hang on and pray as soon as the horse goes into a trot."

Still in my Gary Cooper mode, I allowed, "It ain't easy, that's for sure." Mark would now be howling.

"I'm sorry", she said as she shook her bangs away from her eyes. "Listen to me going on and on. I should be more professional."

"Don't worry. Let's walk this horse a bit."

As we walked up the trail, Ranger Cougar told me that she was on "routine patrol." She then inquired if I had seen the three Australians. I told her that they must be far ahead on the trail by now. As she remounted, she thanked me again. "Thank god it was you. If it was those Australian boys, now that would have been embarrassing." Digesting the comment, I no longer felt like Gary Cooper. As she pushed the horse into a walk, she turned and told me to let her know if I saw anything unusual. I replied, "Like three good-looking, young Australian men?" She blushed again, smiled, and waved.

The Milky Way arced like a haze over my clearing. I dumped more kindling and larger branches onto my cook fire and leaned back against a lodgepole pine. A coyote yipped in the distance and I thought of my sleeping family.

"Good, a hot bed tonight!" The voice scared me out of my drowsing.

Two thin figures approached with their hands held palms open in front of them.

"Don't worry. We come in peace," they said almost in unison. They looked like brothers. Both slightly short, with long, blond, greasy hair tied back in pony tails, narrow faces, sharp chins, and pale blue eyes under the thin blond eyebrows. Each wore a dirty T-shirt and long gray pants.

They did not approach me or offer a handshake. Instead, they sat gently and easily on the far side of the fire with straight backs and crossed legs. There was nothing hostile or scary about these sudden

169

visitors. Instead, it was as though I had been visited by two yoga instructors who had not bathed in several days.

They stared at the glowing embers for a full minute as though it was a new experience. Then, they introduced themselves. Thor and Tam, short for Tamarack. I was tempted, but not quick witted enough, to make up my own nom de guerre, like Stone or Riffle or Zeus, but instead just gave my first name and told them that I was from back East.

Thor responded, "The forest has eyes."

For some reason, this statement irritated me, "What the hell does that mean? You sound like a nature documentary."

Thor flinched slightly. "I just mean, we've been watching you for a while. We could tell you were safe to approach."

"Why is that?"

Tam spoke up, "It was just your manner, your approach. You took the time to listen to that thrush. You watched a mountain bluebird for a long time. And you had a fire."

As I listened, I started to think that Tam was a young woman, but I couldn't be sure. Her T-shirt did not reveal a hint of bosom, but her voice was somewhat high pitched and slightly breathy, and she moved in an indefinably feminine way.

My fire turned out to be important. They admitted that they had not enjoyed a fire for a couple of weeks. Thor announced proudly that they were camping "outlaw" on a rise slightly upstream. They had been hassled earlier in the summer by a Park Ranger and could not light a fire for fear of being discovered.

"Yeah," Tam added, "We were threatened by Casssaannnnnddrraaah. That fat bitch. She fell off her horse today, the idiot. I watched you help her."

DON'T YOU WANT TO BE AN OUTLAW?

Given my conflicted feelings toward Park Rangers, I surprised myself by saying: "Oh, she seems like a nice person. She's just doing her job."

This riled Tam. "Just doing her job? She can't even ride a horse. Doing her job, that's the problem. Well, what's your job, Mr. Back East?" I laughed and told them.

"So, you're really one with the machine. That must be such a drag. Soooo boring." Eyes brightening, Tam took a breath, "Hey, you're part of the problem, not part of the solution." She seemed proud of this philosophical nugget, smiled, and added, "You see, Thor and I choose to live free."

I was tired and in no mood for diplomacy, "So you're two white kids living as monkeywrenching flower children?"

Thor turned to Tam, "Hey he knows Abbey, he's cool," and laughed.

The tension cut, we talked more about their undercover summer in the Yellowstone backcountry. They had left a community college in Grand Rapids, spent the winter dodging authorities in Big Bend National Park, and then hitched up to Yellowstone in June. Tam added, "We live off the land, wild edibles along with some rice we pack in."

Thor cut in, "And handouts. If you have any extra food, we'd really appreciate it."

I pulled out a pouch of freeze-dried fettuccini alfredo, which I had not dared open in three years, and a couple of well-aged ramen noodle packages and tossed them to Thor. The two scooped up the offerings as though they were jewels.

I warned, "Watch out, that fettuccini may be dangerous."

"Hey, it looks good to me," Thor smiled, revealing surprisingly white, straight teeth, "Thanks man."

Tam rose, leaned over and kissed Thor on the top of his head. My gender suspicions seemed confirmed. Tam circled the fire toward me while staring off into the wilderness. Then Tam slowly reached for my shoulder, looked directly into my eyes, and said, "You know what the Boss sings, 'don't you want to be an outlaw?'"

I rose, not nearly as gracefully as Tam, and said, "The one thing I know is that I'm tired. I'm going to bed."

Tam responded, "Hey, that's cool. But, can we use your fire?"

"Sure."

"Thor, I'll spread it out if you get the sleeping bag."

As I reached for the zipper on my tent, I turned and watched Tam spreading out the fire coals gently with a long stick and then scraping a layer of dirt over them.

She turned and saw me staring. "This way, we can sleep in a nice warm bed. You know that U2 song about finding a warm place?"

"No, I don't. I'm more of a Woodstock guy."

"Woodstock? Christ, U2 and Springsteen are about as far back as I can go."

"Not me. 'Tin soldiers and Nixon coming...'"

To my surprise, she completed the verse in a pleasing soprano, "We're finally on our own."

"I would have loved to live during that time. Dylan, Joni, Jimi, Janis. But, no, I had to be a child of the nineties. How boring."

172

"It wasn't as great as it sounds. Today is probably better in some ways."

"Woodstock would have been awesome. How about Richie Havens bringing the sun?" The soprano broke forth, "Freeeeedom!"

Tam's enthusiasm made me feel even more tired. "Well, the revolution continues. Keep fighting. I'm going to bed." The sound of my tent's zipper broke the silence.

I fell asleep immediately, but was wakened soon thereafter by rustling, low grunting, a soft groan, a soprano climax, and Thor's shout, "I'm just a cool rockin' daddy in the USA!"

Even in this age of fluid gender identity, I was pretty sure now that Tam was female.

After falling back to sleep, I was visited by strange dreams. Bruce Springsteen was riding a horse. Cassandra Cougar was touching my shoulder and singing. Skinny nude women danced around a fire, moaning. A coyote danced with the women and, then, it was all coyotes dancing and howling. Slowly, it was just one coyote with its head held up toward the moon and making a loud munching sound. I woke with dull light illuminating the tent.

Looking into my tent was the homeliest moose I have ever seen. Since all moose are homely, that's saying something. This cow had a broken, off-center jaw that jutted to the left while her tongue hung to the right. It seemed a perversion, and I wondered why I was lying on the cold ground in Yellowstone when I could have been warmly curled next to my wife.

There was no sign of Thor or Tam. Except for the neatly smoothed dirt, it was as though the two skinny blonds were a dream. I decided to catch some brookies for breakfast then, hike to a pool warmed by a thermal spring for a long soak. I needed to regain some peace.

I wasn't surprised when I heard Thor's voice in the twilight, "We come in peace."

Tam was excited. "And AWAC is coming soon!"

Who was AWAC? Thor and Tam explained that the initials stood for Andrew Walden Alexander Canford. Tam continued, "You'll see, he's the real deal."

As if on cue, a figure rode in and tied up a small horse a hundred yards away in an aspen grove. As he walked closer, I saw that he was carrying something on his shoulder and wearing a sport coat.

Thor called, "AWAC! You brought meat, good man."

Sure enough, a tall, slim man dressed in a battered Harris Tweed jacket, white sneakers, and worn jeans bowed slightly at the greeting. A Cincinnati Reds baseball cap covered some of his curly reddish-gray hair, and he carried a large bloody chunk of meat on his shoulder.

"Good evening. My name is Andrew. Only young ruffians call me AWAC. I hear that you are a judge. Thor and Tam speak highly of you." It was a voice more at home on the Yale campus than in the wilderness.

He held out his right hand while his left balanced what appeared a quarter of a cow. The grip was firm as I looked at his eagle-like nose and thin lips. AWAC was not handsome, but he certainly was arresting.

"Do you terribly mind if we cook this bison roast over your fire?"

"Bison?"

"Yes, it should be nice and fresh. I shot it today."

"Shot it?"

"Yes, with a bow of course. Any rifle shot would alert the authorities. There simply is nothing quite as good as a bison tenderloin. Of course, we can wash it down with this nice cabernet." He lifted an expensive bottle of Livingstone Cellars from his right jacket pocket. "Do you happen to have a corkscrew? We should let this breathe. In the meantime, I thought we might sip some of this and get acquainted." From his left jacket pocket, AWAC produced a fifth of scotch.

I was amazed and sputtered, "Where, Andrew, did you get this stuff?"

"Oh, I liberated it from the Bear's Den Bar at the Old Faithful Snow Lodge. I doubt if they will even miss it."

Tam excitedly broke in, "I told you he was the real deal. Let's drink."

Who was I to disagree? The scotch looked delicious. It was a 16-year-old Lagavulin single malt. A bottle that I could not afford since having children.

As he poured a generous slug into my Sierra cup, AWAC added, "I only liberate Lagavulin. You can almost taste the heather and smell the North Sea when you sip it."

The bison roasted on a spruce spit and smelled heavenly as I sipped the Scottish heather.

After pouring a third shot into my cup, Andrew helped himself and handed the bottle to Thor. By this point, Thor and Tam had apparently lost their cups and took turns drinking straight from the bottle. Meanwhile Andrew smiled and talked. He grew up in Connecticut. To his father's dismay, he had not attended Yale. Instead he was an English major at Williams College and earned an MBA at Harvard. Then, he explained, followed his "lost decades" of holding jobs and earning money. After his second bitter divorce and during a business trip in 1998, he visited Yellowstone and fell in love with the country. "I was born a century too late, and all of that." Ever since, he spent his summers breaking most laws in the Greater Yellowstone ecosystem and winters living with "a couple of lovely, lonely ranch widows in Paradise Valley and White Sulphur Springs."

The tenderloin was delicious. As I chewed, I never thought of the magnificent shaggy beasts that symbolize the American West. "And," Andrew noted, "you must agree that this California cabernet is a good pairing with such a flavorful meat."

I asked how he managed to hunt bison and avoid such rangers as Cassandra Cougar.

"Ah, Miss Cougar. She reminds me of that country song— unfortunately, Richard, country music is all they seem to play out here—I think it goes: 'ain't no curves like hers on them downtown streets'."

This brought forth an immediate slurred response from Tam, "Watch out, AWAC, or you're going to miss your booty call tonight. Poor, porky Cassaaandraah. Shit, she's probably all alone thinking about those Australian boys."

Andrew's response reminded me of what a strange world I had entered, "Well, Tam, I would never want to miss a lovely night with you. So, I will not speak a word more about the any National Park Service ranger."

"Good." Tam rose, removed the elastic holding her ponytail and shook her head. "Now, AWAC, sing one of your old songs. I just love to hear you sing."

Andrew hummed at first and then began to slowly sing in a surprisingly rich baritone, "Scotch and soda, mud in your eye, ..."

It was an old song. I remembered the Kingston Trio singing it in my youth. Andrew, I thought, must be a few years older than me if he knew this tune.

Tam began to dance slowly around the fire as Andrew continued, "Dry martini, jigger of gin, Oh, what a spell you've got me in...." Thor and Andrew watched her sway and were plainly entranced. But it seemed perverse to me, and I glanced away. With her skinny arms held high and her sharp, narrow face, she reminded me of some homely, adolescent girl trying to be alluring. But then I looked at her perfect smile and those pale blue eyes. If the eyes are a window to the soul, her soul was not unattractive. You could plainly see the searching, the excitement, and, yes, the freedom.

She continued to sway. Andrew rose, held his arms out toward her, and finished the song, "Give me lovin', baby, I feel high."

By the time that the fire burned down and ground was leveled for the threesome, I was safely in my tent. Luckily, the magic of scotch, wine, and bison sent me to a quick, dreamless sleep without a thought of the outside sleeping arrangements. In the morning, only Andrew remained.

He was cooking breakfast when I rose. I didn't ask where he had obtained the eggs and sausage. I just ate and enjoyed.

But I was bothered, so I asked, "What is your relationship with Tam?"

He didn't directly respond. "Ah, my friend, you do not know the half of it. They are lost souls in this modern world, but aren't we all?"

This Buddha-like response didn't thrill me. "But, come on Andrew, you must be close to thirty years older than them."

"I suppose you can be excused for being judgmental. After all, you are a judge." Andrew laughed at his play on words. "You might work on being a little more flexible, no? Age is just a number. At heart, we are all children. Some of us are just children grown old. Try that sausage—it is flavored with fennel and sage."

I gave up and ate the sausage. It was delicious.

Later we hiked over to a small creek that wound through a meadow. We took turns casting for small trout and talked of books recently read and current politics. Andrew was thoughtful, insightful, informed, and an easy companion.

After a half mile, the creek split into three very small channels that were not worth fishing. We walked back to the camp, and Andrew offered to help me pack up.

"No thanks, but thank you for a fine morning, Andrew."

"Without exaggeration, it has been my pleasure. You are fine company. Take good care and send my regards to the modern world." With that Andrew Walden Alexander Canford turned and headed off toward the aspen grove that secreted his horse.

As I hiked out, I heard a horse approaching. Actually, it was two horses. Ranger Cougar was riding tall in the saddle accompanied by a male ranger armed with a Glock sidearm and a military rifle in a scabbard.

DON'T YOU WANT TO BE AN OUTLAW?

I stepped aside, "Good afternoon, Ranger."

"Hi there," Cassandra Cougar said, "I think you're scheduled to head out today. Have you seen anything unusual?"

"Unusual? What do you mean?"

"Someone reported a slaughtered buffalo up the Bechler. Have you seen anything suspicious?"

I bought time by feigning incredulity. "Someone killed a bison and cut it up?"

"Yeah, that's the report. It was an elk a couple of weeks ago. Can you believe it? So, have you come across anything unusual?"

I thought of Thor, Tam, and Andrew. I didn't hesitate. "No, just a peaceful trip, lots of trout and some mountain bluebirds."

Cassandra Cougar smiled. She was a handsome woman, even if she did need to hold on at a trot. Her bulked-up companion looked at me with a dull, suspicious stare and slowly nodded. This lug, I thought, would be no match for AWAC.

The horses walked along. I returned to the trail. All the way back to the trailhead, I never thought about bears. Instead, one memory kept reoccurring: holding Jess in bed and being interrupted as my two boys charged into our room on Christmas morning.

Chapter Seventeen: *As Darkness Rolls Away*

The aging brick building that houses the Jamaica Plain VA Hospital radiates despair. I am here to visit my friend Jack, who is dying all too slowly of lung cancer. This is not my strength. I avoid death, or its suggestion, whenever I can. But I feel an obligation. I leave the cold sun of February to head down a long corridor to the room he shares with a prone man talking nonsense. Jack wakes when I walk in. He recognizes me, croaks out a hello, and asks, "Is it Spring yet?"

"No," I reply, "not yet. The stripers aren't running yet. You'll have to wait for them."

"Hah!" he replies and drifts back into a semi-conscious state. As he lies there breathing noisily, he unconsciously lifts his hands and makes motions with his long fingers as if tying a fly. Then his hands drop to the bed and twitch.

I sit with him and remember a woman who knew us both. Observing Jack's worn wardrobe and his small apartment filled with fly-tying materials and stray cats, she whispered to me, "You're lucky that you have a day job, or you'd have turned out like Jack."

Jack rouses after a while, and we talk about the Red Sox. But he can't keep his thoughts straight and asks, "Is it Spring yet?"

Finally, another friend arrives for the vigil, and I slip out. Jack clasps my hand but can't remember my name. I kiss him on the cheek and head home.

Once home, I remember a photograph that I hung in my office when I was a federal prosecutor. I crouch down as I enter the storage room under the landing of the old mill that is my home. Brushing away cobwebs and a few mice droppings, I drag out the cardboard box containing a bunch of framed pictures. There is the photo, nicely matted with a metal frame. I take it out and get a damp paper towel to remove the dust from the glass. I look at the photo with a smile and pour a glass of red wine and raise it. "Here's to sunnier days, Jack." I prop it on the counter and lean back in my chair.

I study the photograph more closely. We look so damn young. Well, at least George and I do. Jack, with an Old Gold dangling from his fingers, seems to have survived a few late nights. There we are, arms around each other's backs, at the "Three Dollar" bridge on the Madison, with the mountains rearing up in the background and the clear evening sunlight slanting in, fully outfitted for wading the river, and with a variety of smiles on our faces: Jack's slightly world weary as though he has done this so many times before but is looking forward to it again, George's direct and sincere with a hint of impatience to get casting, and mine as big and naive as a toddler. The differences in our fishing vests are instructive. George's pockets are bulging with fly boxes, the material stained from many a trip; Jack's vest barely exists, the flimsy green mesh so torn that he equates it with a Frederick's of Hollywood tear-away nightie; and mine is a shockingly white L.L. Bean beginner number with barely an item within.

In the picture I proudly grasp my new purchase for this Western trip, a fat brown fiberglass rod that Orvis now would be embarrassed to acknowledge. George already sports a fancy Sage graphite while the tip of Jack's nondescript rod broke off earlier that summer—Jack assures us that it casts just as well four inches shorter. Given our posture and positions, it is clear that, despite his equipment shortcomings, Jack is the master. He is the wise brown trout, George the experienced and energetic rainbow, and I the happy and gullible cutthroat.

AS DARKNESS ROLLS AWAY

Beginnings are one of life's sweetest fruits. This was not my first fly fishing foray. I labored at casting for bluegills on a weedy New England mill pond after many evenings reading outdoor magazine articles. My technique and knowledge, however, were non-existent. Jack and George generously showed me the way.

That way led to Mosquito Gulch. The name is not a work of fiction but rather an actual small, soggy clearing hard against the Madison's South Fork and six bumpy, twisting dirt miles southwest of West Yellowstone. Mosquito Gulch has nothing to recommend it other than a few lodgepole pines with grizzly claw scars and the important fact that one can camp there undisturbed and without paying one penny of tribute to the bothersome Forest Service or National Park. Jack had discovered this buggy depression and encouraged George and me to join him in this no-rent locale. As I have indicated, I was gullible and naive and pitched my small tent immediately. Jack marveled at the luxury of a one-man tent with aluminum poles; he, in contrast, simply left a third-hand sleeping bag next to an ill-defined fire pit adorned with open cans of partially consumed Vienna sausages. He claimed that sleeping next to the cold embers warded off the bears, but he did admit to some concern about being stepped on by a night-time moose wandering toward the stream. Surveying the scene, the more experienced George threatened to abandon us and take up with some overweight Montana barmaid.

At least we did not attempt to cook at the aptly named Mosquito Gulch. We would return to our sleeping bags late in the evening well-fortified by alcohol, sleep with surprising soundness, awake to the frosty Montana morning, and tumble into the mud-covered rental car for a return trip to town in order to consume greasy eggs and watery coffee at whatever cafe had a restroom with running water and a toilet. Not to trumpet my advanced age, but this was when West Yellowstone did not sport its current paved roads, art galleries, or decent coffee joints. The dirt streets contained pot holes that could—and did—swallow Volkswagens; late-night laundromats received many a visit by strolling bears; the Stagecoach Inn was the only classy bar, and even there one was likely to run into a fist-waving drinker sporting a baseball cap with the logo "Instant Asshole, Just Add Alcohol."

After breakfast I paced, eager to begin fishing. It was an eagerness known mostly to the novice: donning clammy waders, slipping on slimy rocks, walking long distances under a blistering sun, casting endlessly and mostly fruitlessly, and hooking large amounts of vegetation with my unruly backcasts. Jack, however, would leisurely stroll the streets, visit with numerous friends for infuriatingly lengthy periods, and assure me that the "fishing doesn't get good until after noon." That left me time to purchase flies the size and pattern of which Jack would marvel. "I've never seen one quite like that" or "I guess you're after *really* big trout." Jack would then pass me a couple of his magnificently tied pheasant hoppers and quietly suggest that I try casting them first.

And try I did. Although we fished many rivers, it is the Madison I remember most. In the Slide Inn stretch, my two taller and steadier companions propped me between them, linked arms and together we crossed the deep, rushing current. My feet slipped frantically on the rocks, but the two steady tanks on each side steadied me until, in deeper water, only my toes brushed a boulder or two and, then, I was hoisted onto the far shore. After surging out of the torrent, neither Jack nor George mentioned the obvious truth: they were lugging deadwood.

Most often, we fished less challenging currents downstream. George would take one side of the river and tempt many a rainbow and brown. Jack and I would fish the opposite bank. As I now

184

reflect on the scene, Jack was remarkably patient and kind. While Jack usually was rigged up within seconds, he would wait as I clumsily tied cinch knots. He let me fish the bank first and then followed along. "Short casts, just keep moving. You're doing great Richard." When I suggested that we "hopscotch" up the bank, fishing different areas, Jack declined and saying that he would fish the same stretch. Jack, who could never resist even the worst joke, reassuringly added, "Don't worry there are plenty of fish. Did you hear about the guy who entered the restaurant that advertised 'Breakfast Any Time' and ordered French Toast in the Renaissance? Just keep moving. You're doing great." To my amazement, after I covered a pocket with a pheasant hopper and did not raise a fish, Jack followed, flicking the same pattern in seemingly the same water, catching trout after trout.

We fished late into the evening. We laughed, joked, and walked miles under the Montana sun. When it got too dark to see the fly on the water, we met back at the car and compared notes. George, a hard-charging fisherman, always caught a high number. Jack would raise nearly a hundred trout and land about a third of them. Lighting another Old Gold, he would look down almost shyly and say, "I love fooling them and watching the beautiful things rise. You don't hook all of them, but I always try to equal Ted Williams's life-time batting average." I must have been a better person back then, for despite few fish and many a tangle, I never felt jealous or even slightly humiliated, only happy and content to be in the company of such wonderful friends.

One's first encounters often take on a golden glow that make later forays pale in comparison. Not so with Jack. Jack had the Peter Pan quality to be forever as young, exciting, and exasperating as an eleven-year-old. Every trip, and there were many, was an adventure—for good or bad. Driving Jack to fishing destinations was rarely easy. On a New York highway near our Beaverkill destination, Jack screamed for us to stop. After argument and dangerous automotive maneuvers, Jack sprinted out of the car to pick up a not so recently road-killed woodchuck. "A woodchuck's fur makes the best caddis," Jack explained. Said animal, with its strong scent, then accompanied us in the backseat for the rest of the trip. While Jack was a challenge in a car, he was a danger in a boat as he always insisted on getting "just a little closer." The result was many a dent from the North Atlantic rocks or a grounding near Florida's Content Keys or a stranding on the Merrimack's Joppa Flats. All of this was done, again and again, with joy and laughter.

Jack died two days later. The wake was actually fun. Old acquaintances hugged and shared stories. But, after the casket was lowered and all dispersed, there remained an emptiness.

Now with two children and family duties, I fish only in snippets. Helping with biology homework, shuttling boys to football practice and riding lessons, finding time for a quick date with my wife—it all makes extended fishing adventures, at least for this New Age male, an impossibility. But as the weather warms, the desire still burns. I now quietly sneak out alone in the earliest morning hours and fish as the darkness of an early summer night rolls away and light first touches the North American continent. It is the most optimistic of hours, and I sometimes think of one of my most optimistic friends. I look out onto the water in the estuaries that make up the massive salt marsh of northern Massachusetts and New Hampshire and await the large, almost scary, swirl of a striped bass. In this setting, I am reminded of Robert Traver's missive that we fish to be in the beautiful places where wild fish live. But Traver forgot one thing. We fish not only for the beauty, but oddly enough, given that fishing is an inherently solitary sport, we fish for the companionship. On those early mornings I am almost convinced that Jack is nearby in the fog casting and once again saying, with his constant good humor, "Any minute now, Richard. They're going to be here any minute." And so, I cast again into the sweeping tide.

I look back at that picture. The long Montana summer evening is beginning, the caddis will be dancing around the Madison's rocks, we are ready to go and have no place to be other than with ourselves. Damn, we were young.

Chapter Eighteen: *The Peaceable Kingdom*

We mirror some L.L. Bean cover. The smiling husband, beautiful wife, and two handsome sons striding off with packs and rods into an American outdoor icon: Yellowstone. The light of early evening has started to slant, and the temperature cools under a cloudless sky. Of course, it's not that simple.

Closer inspection reveals that wife Jess is not carrying a rod or anything remotely related to fishing. She sees no reason to be armed with anything other than a water bottle and a quick energy protein bar. Jess happily denounces fly fishing and calls her husband "a drainage guy" who she has to drag up the mountains to view the peaks. Past efforts to introduce her to the sport have met with humorous disasters or a level of discomfort that has easily outweighed any slight interest in tempting a trout. Her only purpose here is a bit of a cardio workout and, more important, to be with her sixteen- and eighteen-year-old sons.

In the heated throws of initial romance, she good naturedly gave the sport a try. After derricking cutthroat into flight when they slowly sipped her hopper and spearing her own back with a 1/0 hook of a Lefty's Deceiver during a windy hunt for stripers, any small thrill was gone. After all, it is hard to rationalize endless hours slopping along a cold stream or waking before dawn to brush away clouds of mosquitoes in the hope of feeling a strong tug on your line. Now I usually depart alone with her perennial request, "Just don't hurt yourself." A reminder that I am a rapidly aging American male.

The eighteen-year-old is also free of fishing paraphilia. Not the surly, hardened young adult I often see in the court dock, Rich possesses a kindness and sweetness that makes a parent occasionally quake for his wellbeing. His first loves are family, nature, and Yellowstone. His only interest in trout is to appreciate their beauty and to make sure that they survive their encounter with an artificial fly cast by someone else. Although he proclaims to new acquaintances and on college applications to love fly fishing, he does not. What he loves is to hike along a stream with his father and enjoy the sounds, sights, and companionship. This has not changed since I first brought him along a Western stream when he was six. He happily hopped and balanced among the loose river rocks, forded the stream holding his father's hand, and knelt beside the creek to fill my hat with water as if straining it. Each time I would catch a trout, he would pop the dripping hat on his head, run up the bank, lightly touch the fish with a moist hand, and wish it well. Then back to the water, straining and daydreaming.

I can count on the strapping sixteen-year-old, who is quickly exceeding the height of my taller, elegant wife, to carry more than his fair share of rod, tackle, and water. Robert sets the pace for us and strides with a purpose. Like his brother, he loves the wild, but he is on a mission. Of course, the mission of any adolescent may be fraught with complexity and, perhaps, psychological baggage. Today, however, it is simple: the elusive grayling.

He claims to friends, particularly of the female variety, to be an avid and accomplished fly fisherman. That may be a bit of a stretch. He reads the water like a pro, but his cast is still ragged, and he turns to me for the more sophisticated knots. Providing subtle parental instruction is not easy. Recently we walked up a fine creek pitching dry flies to fair-sized trout. After Robert missed three good fish in a row and used increasingly colorful language, I suggested that he was setting the hook too quickly. In the next pool, he waited as a particularly large rainbow rose. He set the hook perfectly. To his surprise, the fish charged upstream, sped to an undercut bank and promptly broke off. He gently placed the rod and dangling line against a driftwood log and announced that he was through with fishing for the day. As we ate sandwiches on the same log, I laughed and truthfully told him that I could never have landed the rainbow. Robert did not join in the laughter. I pulled out a small Turk's Tarantula and rebuilt his leader—just in case he wanted to join me in fishing after lunch. Sure enough, he proceeded to catch plenty of nice trout, and we happily hiked out of the stream as a killdeer called.

Both boys have never seen a grayling, and so our destination is Cascade Lake. Jess also has never seen a grayling; but, unlike the sons, has never expressed the slightest interest in observing, never mind catching, this unique and now-threatened species. Still, the three-mile hike is relatively flat and cuts through flower-filled fields and beautiful spurs of spruce. The smiles on our faces are genuine.

We round a corner and find the sixteen-year-old son standing like a statue. There is nothing like a large bison bull, wallowing in the middle of the trail, to pull the starch out of a boy. These bulls in the backcountry are truly impressive and unpredictable at best.

We stare at the massive beast. I comment on its beauty. Jess responds, "My life would be fine if I never saw a buffalo again." The boys disagree and claim that their mother only holds this antipathy because of a particularly lusty bison that, during last year's rut, brushed her car window and proceeded to lick it repeatedly while grunting vigorously. The eighteen-year-old son opines, "Mom, that bison really liked you." Both boys laugh.

Jess smiles and says, "That was truly disgusting. Now be careful taking a detour around this beast."

The boys begin a long detour aiming to regain the trail at the next small ridge.

Jess looks at me, "Every time we are out here, I am reminded how different we are."

One is never completely free of the past, and her statement makes me a bit nervous, "An old girlfriend once said something like that to me, and the relationship didn't end well."

Jess laughs, takes my hand, and squeezes. Never one to hide or moderate her opinion, my wife adds, "That girl was a fool. But, then, who isn't at that age?" She states this with her usual certainty.

I look at her as she watches the boys' progress. Jessica Stills Cameron, with long dark hair now streaked with silver, beautiful pale face, and blue-green eyes, is a true Scottish beauty. With her height, regal bearing, and occasional war-like attitude, there is no doubt that she is from the Highlands. When particularly upset, I envision her on some barren hillside, in the front ranks of her clan, bearing a broadsword, and about to descend upon the soon-to-be-vanquished enemy.

"Well," I reply, "that foolish girl is happily married to some rich venture capitalist and she travels around the world buying art."

Jess wrinkles her brow in mock concentration, tilts her head, and says with a hint of a smile, "Maybe she was not so foolish."

Then, regaining her usual definitiveness, the Scottish warrior states, "It would be boring if we were alike."

"I am blessed to have found you," I reply.

Seizing the moment, Jess adds, "But you still could go clothes shopping with me sometimes. I value your advice."

I moan, she makes a face of exaggerated frustration, and we follow the boys.

The path is well worn and wide in places. After another mile, I slow to let my wife catch up and then take her hand. As we walk, she remembers, "You wanted to hold my hand on our first date."

"Of course, I did. I was strolling through Cambridge on a warm spring evening with a beautiful woman. But, no, you crossed your arms. What a prude."

"It *was* our first date. I didn't even know you."

"You said I looked like a Republican."

"Well, you did! That blue suit, white shirt, and red tie. I wasn't holding hands with some right winger. And you were so nervous. You were clapping your hands."

"All the more reason to hold my hand."

She smiles, "Remember the parking lot you walked me back to?"

"Yeah, the one in the fancy hotel. We were both parked there."

"It was filled with BMWs and Mercedes and my old Volvo, and I asked you which car was yours. You pointed to that rusty Toyota pickup parked in the corner. I almost laughed."

"That was your first tip-off. You should have married some guy with lots of money."

"Don't be silly. I waited my whole life to meet you."

It may be typical, even banal, marital talk. But it leaves me feeling closer to my wife.

The trail narrows as it ascends a small hill. I let go of her hand, and we resume walking in a single file.

We reach the small lake at the perfect time. The wind has settled for the evening and the mirror surface is pocked with an occasional rising fish. An osprey wheels about her large nest as a marmot whistles its warning. We are alone in this peaceable kingdom.

The osprey plunges into the still lake. Flaps its wings, and lifts with a fish. The craziness of this spinning rock seems so far away.

My wife and older son lounge on a huge fallen Douglas fir while the sixteen-year-old puts his back into casting a parachute Adams as far out as possible. I tell him that he need not cast such a distance. He ignores me, walks up the shoreline, and catches a grayling on his third cast. He is excited and amazed by its nearly phosphorescent dorsal fin. We all cluster around to watch him release this rarity. After he catches a couple more, I ask if his brother can borrow the rod. Ripe with success, he graciously hands over the rod and encourages his older brother. With a little help, the fly floats on the smooth surface until a grayling jumps over the fly and takes it on its way down. It is a fat ten-incher and he gently strokes the fish as it is released. His younger brother claps him on the back with congratulations.

I walk up the shore a bit and pull out line from my rod. I see a slight swirl and cast. I am surprised when I hear my wife say, "You are a beautiful caster." There is a tenderness in her voice. I did not realize that she had followed me up the shore and never had heard her compliment anything about fishing, never mind her husband as a fly fisher. I try self-deprecation, but she repeats, "No, you are beautiful to watch."

Maybe it's twenty years of marriage or the obvious sincerity in her tone, but I feel a jolt of pleasure mixed with a shot of surprise. This is the same woman who no longer visits my courtroom because of the ritual when the judge enters. Striding onto the bench as a rookie judge, I noticed a commotion in the audience. Two burly court officers were bent over a seated form while jurors,

194

lawyers, clients, victims, and other observers stood patiently. Then a familiar voice, "I am not standing for him. He's just my husband!" Ever since a governor nominated me to the bench, she has diligently accepted her domestic responsibility of keeping my ego in check. So, I glance over at this wonderful woman with a smile and, of course, miss the take.

I laugh. Cast again and feel full of love. I catch a short, fat cutthroat and then a grayling.

"Hey, let me try now." She hasn't picked up a rod in fifteen years. The boys are now gathered to witness their mother casting. Her backcast drops and becomes firmly hooked on a monkey flower. The younger son strides over and fixes the problem. Another cast, but no fish rise to the fly. I suggest casting out just a bit farther. "Remember, take it back to 12 o'clock, stop, and forward."

I am firmly hooked. The size 16 dry fly impales my lower lip. But my wife is still casting, whipping the rod back and forth, looking behind her to see if some pesky plant has again snagged her backcast. I am at her side, on my knees, grasping the line so that it cannot be tugged further. The boys are laughing loudly and spluttering, "Stop, Mom, stop."

Finally, she asks what is so funny. Blood is dripping onto my hand and the boys are laughing so hard that they cannot catch their breath. When she sees the problem, she is startled, yet can't help joining in the laughter. She claims that she is laughing out of anxiety, but anyone can hear the note of hilarity.

The sixteen-year-old is fresh off an outdoor emergency training course and expertly rips the fly from my lip. He claims that he backed it out gently, but I feel one with the trout. My lip quickly expanding, I assure everyone that I am fine. And, I am.

With long, light strides, we head back. The sun is near the
hilltops and our shadows are absurdly long in the evening light. It
is close enough to dusk that we talk loudly to warn away any bears.
The boys tease their mother and marvel at the beauty of a grayling.
Everyone laughs when I begin to slur my words as the lip grows.
The bison has disappeared. It is smooth sailing. We reach the last
patch of trees in the twilight. In the shadow of the spruce, it is dark.
Then we emerge to the last small field and our car. We drive off
toward Dunraven Pass and toward a warm, well-lighted place and
dinner.

Chapter Nineteen: *What Carries You Out*

The Milky Way and the shooting stars made the ten-mile hike, which gained four thousand heart-pounding feet of elevation, almost worth it. At midnight, we dragged our inflated sleeping pads out of the tents and lay on our backs watching the incredible light show. My lifelong friend Mark, my twenty-two-year old son Robert, and I whooped with each meteor that sprayed its track along the black sky. Up on this high mountain shelf, the Big Dipper seemed almost within reach.

We were on Homer Youngs Peak on the Montana side of the Beaverhead Range. Why Homer's last name did not include an apostrophe remained a mystery. I thought about this sort of trivia to take my mind off of humping a pack up a scree-filled pitch appropriately named "Satan's Slide." Once up the Slide I doubled over trying to catch my breath. I knew I was out of my league when my twenty-year-old son, lugging a backpack considerably larger and heavier than mine, announced, in a voice filled with enthusiasm and concern, "You're doing great, Dad. Just take your time. Make sure to find the handholds in the rocks as we climb up this stretch."

Handholds in the rocks? I gazed at the Beaverhead Valley below and wondered how I had been talked into this adventure. As I looked up the steep cliff face with its handholds, I remembered that very near here Merriweather Lewis had practically skipped across the gentle Lemhi Pass to become the first white American to cross the Continental Divide. That thought didn't help. I changed mental channels and wondered when it was that a son takes over the role from the father of being the guide, the protector, and the cheerleader.

Mark was not helping matters by adding, in an equally cheerful and solicitous tone, "Come on, Rich, we can do this. This is the steepest part. After this it will be easy." It was one thing to be encouraged by a strapping young son, but it was almost humiliating for my childhood friend to be so concerned about my physical shape that he resorted to lying.

I reminded Mark that he was full of shit because he had no idea what the trail was like beyond this point. We had never climbed this peak before. "You're right," he responded breezily, "but, if it is steeper ahead, then we are completely fucked." Our laughter was interrupted by my son, "Come on guys, we're burning daylight. Just take it slow."

Mark and I smiled at each other, and I answered, "Don't worry, we'll take it very slow."

The truth was that no one had talked me into this. I had been looking forward to the challenge, if not the pain. While lying in the Massachusetts General Hospital after extensive prostate surgery and listening to hot-shot doctors grimly pronounce that the aggressive and lethal cancer had spread to numerous lymph nodes, I resolved to fish the streams of the Beaverhead for native grayling and camp on the Homer Youngs shelf. The next day, I shared this plan with one of the doctors. He repeated, "In four months?" Then, he shook his head, smiled, raised his hands, and said, "Hey, why not?"

My wife, Jess, who was sitting next to my bed in a cramped chair during the conversation, had apparently expected a more cautionary and learned response to what she gently termed my "silly plan." Not one to restrain her opinion, she let it be known. The doctor, armed with impressive titles and degrees and surrounded by a crowd of young interns and other groupies, smiled gently at us, leaned forward toward my wife, and softly said, "One thing I have learned practicing medicine is that while you have life, you should live it." He then touched her hand and lowered his eyes. Jess's face was filled with sympathy and alarm, and she lowered her head. As the doctor left the room, he encouraged his coterie to exit first, turned back at the door, and with a broad grin raised his right thumb. Unfortunately, Jess lifted her head at the same time and caught the doctor's gesture. Her hissed opinion came swiftly, "I know that doctor is renowned, but I swear, he's as ridiculous as you are. He's just another immature boy and he's trying to give you some cover."

"Hey, Jess," I responded, "he's a world-famous surgeon. I think we better follow his advice." She exhaled audibly, turned toward me, wiped at her eyes and we both smiled for the first time in a long time.

We made it to the ten-thousand-foot shelf. Wheezing, I threw off my pack and collapsed onto a field of columbine and bluebells. I looked over at Mark, who, while not as winded, was in a similarly prone position, staring up at the endless blue sky. Even after a year, looking at Mark's familiar face startled me. A while ago he was kicked in the head by a mule.

When I first heard of the accident, I thought that this was some type of celestial payback for owning a 600-acre spread in Wyoming and a remuda of thirty horses. The Bar M Ranch, with its large log home and extensive barns, was envy producing enough. But, no, Mark also owned a remarkable house in Santa Barbara due to earning ridiculous sums as a high flyer in the cable television industry. After selling his company and becoming an early retiree,

199

Mark bought the Wyoming ranch. He justified the expenditure to me, "I made all this money in an industry that won't last another decade. I want to own something that will last at least until Yellowstone erupts or our species goes extinct in about forty years."

Soon I learned how extensive the damage was from the kick and I felt guilty for my initial, glib reaction. Mark had suffered a broken nose, pulverized orbital bone, dented skull, and a demolished jaw. Despite expert care and reconstruction, the left side of his face was dramatically different than the right. His right eye now drooped, as did that corner of his mouth. His right cheekbone was nonexistent, and there was a slight dent near the temple. All of this might have seemed less noticeable on another man, but Mark had been remarkably handsome: tall, slim, wide-shouldered, thick sandy hair, butter-brown eyes, high cheek bones, and strong chin—the whole package. Indeed, in his twenties, he was hired as a television model pitching some breakfast cereal. As a friend, it was sometimes an irritating male beauty, the kind that made women take a second look at him on the street, in a bar, or at an airport, while no one looked twice at my boring mug. His handsome face now remained, but only on one side. It was somewhat like a two-sided theater mask.

We talked of the fishing the day before: Robert's remarkable cast that caught the largest grayling, the beautiful Centennial Valley, the flocks of sandhill cranes and trumpeter swans. Mark paused and said, almost apologetically, "You know, Rich would have loved seeing those swans." He knew my two sons well from extensive visits.

He was absolutely correct that my older son would have been fascinated with the broad, gentle valley filled with waterfowl. I felt guilty that he wasn't with us. I replied, "He has always wanted to see the Centennial Valley ever since reading *The Trumpet of the Swan*. When he was young, we spent two weeks listening to that book on tape as we drove around Yellowstone. He still loves that book." I felt like a lousy and selfish father. I shook my head and faced reality, "But he would have hated those handholds and, particularly, the near vertical climb at the end."

Mark must have sensed my regret and guilt, for he added, "And, don't forget how cold it will be tonight. He wouldn't like that. And he might not be a fan of the dehydrated food on the menu this evening."

I appreciated Mark's subtle kindness and agreed with a nod, "He's probably perfectly content reading, feeding the wood stove, eating a steak dinner, and watching a movie with Jess at the cabin."

We looked at each other and said in unison, "Smart man." Then we laughed.

Mark continued, "You are lucky. You have two fine sons and a wonderful wife."

I agreed and sensed where Mark, who had divorced two wives and was considering marrying a third, was going. "Maybe I should have waited for the right one, like you did. Then, I might have had my own children. But I could never wait. I blame it on that all-boys school we went to. Some beautiful blond with half a brain talks me up and, the next thing I know, boom, I'm married."

"Ah," I replied, "the troubles of the rich."

Mark shifted to one elbow and faced me, "Hey, that's not fair. You and I were scholarship kids at that school. They just felt guilty and let a couple of local yokels onto the ivy campus."

"Mark, you just like the idea of being married. That's why you're thinking about doing it again. Anyway, you know I was a big fan of your second wife Emily."

"Yeah," he acknowledged while swatting away a bee, "she's great. I blew that one. But, man, you are lucky to have such a family."

I laughed, "As Jess says, luck has nothing to do with it. It's just damn hard work."

Still lying down, we directed Robert to pitch the tents and set up the stoves. "This is the way it should be," Mark observed, "we trained the young stud, now he should be taking care of us."

"I'm not so sure about how much training we did. You introduced him to horses, and I showed him a bit about fly fishing. Then he just took off on his own and look at him now: climbing peaks, rodeoing, and fishing circles around us."

"True," Mark replied, "but, at our age, we should take credit for everything, particularly if it is undeserved."

I changed the topic. "I better get up before I fall asleep. Let's go down to the creek and filter some water."

"O.K.," Mark agreed. "Some water would taste good."

"Scotch would taste better."

I knew the comment would get Mark going, and it did. Mark always talked a good health game. One week he was going to be a vegetarian, a few weeks later a vegan, but then a pulled-pork sandwich and a Corona would seduce him. "Water is much healthier for you. It is the perfect drink."

This would be fun. I knew I could crank up my old friend into a righteous tirade, "Not as perfect as a cold beer."

202

Mark huffed, "Beer at ten thousand feet is dangerous to one's health."

I smiled and responded, "What medical school did you attend?"

"Water is so much ...," Mark hesitated, looked at me, and smiled. He knew he had fallen into the same old trap. "Next time, we bring up a couple of Tecates and soak them in this cold stream. They would taste good, and we won't even have to carry them if we sneak them into Robert's pack."

I draped my arm over his shoulder as we came to the stream and said, "I'm lucky to have such a friend."

"Luck," Mark, always wary of mushy sentimentality, replied in his usual quick fashion, "has nothing to do with it. It's just damn hard work."

The next morning, the packs felt heavier. I mentioned this fact to Robert. He reached over, tousled my hair and replied, "At least it is all downhill today." And, so, off we plodded, Robert leading and Mark in the rear.

It was slow going, but uneventful. On the steepest sections we took off our packs, tied them to ropes, and lowered them down. The sun was hot, but it was easier losing, rather than gaining, altitude. The near vertical scramble down the first five hundred yards made the angle of the loose scree at Satan's Slide look almost gentle. We each had a hiking pole and Robert warned, "Follow me, take it slow, and brace your pole in front of you before each step."

Mark and I watched Robert make it to a small outcropping of spruce. "Oh, to be young," I said as I began the descent. Picking my way through the rocks, I made it to the spruce. Robert gave me a one-armed hug. Then, we turned to watch Mark slip when the talus slid, catch himself, and carefully work his way to us.

"Good," Robert grinned, "now let's slowly cut back and forth down the rest of this slope like we were skiing. It's too steep to go straight down."

We watched Robert head off on a forty-five-degree angle and begin his zig-zag down the rocks. I headed off on the same path.

"He's quite a kid, you must be proud," Mark said.

I looked back at Mark and replied, "Oh, I certainly am." The flat rocks began to slide under my right foot and I tried to regain my balance. I heard Mark yell, "I got you," as he leaned forward. Suddenly, he went down and was in motion, brushing past me while falling head first straight downhill. As I lost my balance and fell, I heard the solid sound of Mark's body hitting stone. Using my pole, I righted myself and looked downhill at Mark laying still, his head hard against a large rock. I yelled to Robert and started down to Mark. This time, the entire hillside seemed to slip under my boots as a rockslide threw me down the hill. Robert caught my arm and pack as I slid by.

Robert sat me upright and nervously yelled, "Are you alright?"

I turned away from him and vomited. "I think my left leg got crushed and is broken."

"Sit here, take a sip of this water, and I'll climb up to Uncle Mark."

"I'll come with you."

"Listen to me, Dad. Stay here. I'll be right back with Uncle Mark."

Robert scrambled up to Mark, placed him into a fireman's carry and brought him down to the base of the slide, laying him down in the shade of a Douglas fir. His wilderness training must have kicked in because I watched as Robert cleaned a bad wound to the left side of Mark's forehead, tear his T-shirt into a bandage, and wrap it twice around Mark's head. Then, Robert slapped Mark's cheek hard and yelled into his face. Mark said something softly to Robert and my son began to quickly scramble up to me.

"Is Mark alive?" I asked.

"Alive enough to say 'thank you.'"

I took off my T-shirt so that Robert could lash my pole as a splint on my left leg. He half carried me over to the shade as I hopped slowly with my arm over his shoulder. He gently lowered me so that I could sit next to Mark.

I looked over at Mark. His eyes were open, but slightly crossed, "Mark, how are you?'

"Did we win?" Mark always had been a competitive athlete, and this latest concussion must have sent him back to some long past contest.

"Uncle Mark," Robert raised his voice, "we just got off the mountain. You fell. I'm going for help."

The bandage around Mark's head showed a spreading, bright red stain. "I don't need help, did we win?"

Robert and I discussed his plan. Although we were mostly off the mountain, we were still five miles within the wilderness. We had no cell coverage and no satellite phone. The quickest rescue would be for Robert to run out, borrow some horses from a nearby outfitter he knew, and pack us out to the car.

I assured Robert that we would be fine and kissed him on the cheek. He took off at a quick jog.

"Did we win?"

Mark began to close his eyes. "Hey, Mark, stay awake. You have to stay awake."

"Why?" Mark's left eye focused on me. I could see that he was more aware.

"I don't know. But I think someone with a head injury is not supposed to sleep."

"Where did you go to medical school?" Mark asked with a crooked half smile. The smile filled me with relief. Mark added, "Hey, put a pillow under my head."

"Mark, we don't have a pillow. Let me move my pack under your head." When I lifted his head onto the pack, a rivulet of blood slowly slid down toward his eye. I wiped it away with a handkerchief.

"Christ," Mark continued, "Look at us. What a mess we are. Do you know you pissed your pants?"

I looked down at my gray shorts. Sure enough, my crotch was enveloped by a large wet stain. "I must have filled up the pad."

"You're wearing a pad?"

"Yeah, ever since the surgery. 'Guaranteed complete all-day protection and comfort.'"

Mark groaned and then responded, "Well, they lied. No one can guarantee complete protection or comfort."

I looked again at my crotch. "I guess not. But it's hardly important."

"Christ," he repeated, "Look at us. We are truly pathetic. My head hurts." Then, he closed his eyes.

After a few minutes, I yelled at him to wake up. Mark's eyes opened, and he asked, "Did we win?"

After an hour of my rousing Mark and his groans and babbling, he suddenly clearly asked, "Did you break your leg?"

"Yeah, I think I did. It's swelling up like a beach ball and I can't really feel it." I paused, but wanted to continue the conversation, "You know Mark, Montana always has been hard on me."

Mark gave a soft laugh, "Please, don't tell me the story of Sacagawea on the Greyhound bus again."

"I won't." I said with a smile. "I promise. Still, Montana seems so much harsher than the lush, gentle East or even the rolling fields of Idaho."

Mark answered with almost a sneer, "Yeah, years ago, Wallace Stegner said the same thing, but much more eloquently." I was surprised at Mark's tone because we were always careful not to criticize what was important to each other. Still, I was delighted that he was back among the thinking.

I wanted him to talk, so I asked, "Remember swimming off Sandy Point?"

"Oh, yeah, body surfing the big rollers. The salt water drying on your skin. The mosquitoes and greenheads eating you alive." Mark's eyes were no longer crossed but the entire left side of his face, the good side, was turning a purplish red. "This is one hell of a headache."

I desperately asked, "Remember Alex?" I badly wanted to keep him talking.

Mark's eyes had lost their focus and he responded, "Yeah, I think so. Yeah, of course I do. Good guy, such a sad end. I'll never understand it."

I pressed the conversation, "Do you think we could have helped him more? It still bothers me."

Mark was plainly irritated. "We did help him, over and over."

"I still worry that we could have done something more."

Mark's reply was harsh, "You worry and worry. That's why you never made any money."

I had never heard Mark speak in such a hard tone. Hell, I thought, the head injury is significant.

Mark, then quietly said, "I don't want to think about it now. I just want to close my eyes."

This time I let him. I told myself that maybe a little rest might help. I stared at Mark lying on his back, still, with closed eyes. I thought of my parents and how each had complained of bad headaches and then, suddenly died of brain aneurysms. I shifted my bad leg and told myself that this was no aneurysm, only a nasty smack to the skull. That's right, I repeated to myself again and again, just a real nasty smack to the skull.

After twenty more minutes, Mark opened his eyes and asked, "Hey, did we win?" Then he closed his eyes, breathing heavily.

I heard my son Robert before I saw him. Given the snorting and shouts,

I could tell that he was pushing the horses hard. I rocked Mark back and forth and told him that Robert was coming.

Mark lifted himself by his elbows. "Where is he?"

Then, Robert was in sight and riding a fast-trotting mule. Two other mules trailed. He waved his hat and smiled his big innocent smile. I waved back and kept waving. The outfitter must have let him borrow a Denver Broncos T shirt that clung tightly to his chest and strong arms. I did not feel relief that he had appeared, only pride in what a young, capable man he had become.

I asked Mark if he could see Robert. "Yeah, are those mules he's bringing?"

"That's right. We'll ride them out and get to a hospital."

Mark shook his head, "I am not riding any damn mule. I'm not going to get close to one."

There was the same unfamiliar hardness in Mark's tone. "Look, Mark," I attempted gently, "I know you have always been a quarter horse guy, but we don't have a lot of choices."

He replied with the same harsh certainty, "That's right, quarter horses. No mules."

Robert arrived and was tying up the string of mules. There was no time to negotiate with my concussed friend. So, I switched to my judicial voice, "Listen, we have to get out of here. We don't get to choose what carries us out. It's the mules. Let's get going."

Mark turned to me, and the harshness was gone when he said, "I love it when you talk Judge to me." His left eye was swollen shut, but his right eye sparkled as I looked into his ruined face.

Robert strode up. Perhaps he overheard us, or he might have predicted Mark's reaction, "Gentlemen, your mounts await. Hey, Uncle Mark, I brought some mules just for you."

Mark reached up and gripped my left forearm. I tightly squeezed Mark's forearm in return. I looked at my son's big smile. I wanted to thank him and say much more. But I was filled with emotion—

pride, joy, love, and sorrow for soon leaving this fine earth—and knew that I would cry long and hard if I tried to say anything. So, with my other hand, I reached for Robert's and returned his smile.

THE END

About the Author

A former federal prosecutor and Justice of the Massachusetts Superior Court, Richard E. Welch III has been employed as a rivet packer, a free-lance journalist, a law school professor, and a part-time fly-fishing guide. He is the author of numerous professional articles and short stories in addition to this novel.

He lives with his wife and two sons in Newburyport, Massachusetts and Tetonia, Idaho.

Made in the USA
Middletown, DE
24 September 2019